FROM SEED TO SKILLET

FROM SEED

TO SKILLET

A Guide to Growing, Tending, Harvesting, and Cooking Up Fresh, Healthful Food to Share with People You Love

by JIMMY WILLIAMS and SUSAN HEEGER photographs by ERIC STAUDENMAIER

CHRONICLE BOOKS
SAN FRANCISCO

Text copyright © 2010 by *Jimmy Williams* and *Susan Heeger*.
Photographs copyright © 2010 by *Eric Staudenmaier*.

All rights reserved. No part of this book may be reproduced in any form
without written permission from the publisher.

Library of Congress Cataloging-in-Publication Data available.
ISBN 978-0-8118-7221-8

Manufactured in China.

Designed by *Andrew Schapiro*
Prop and food styling by *Char Hatch Langos*
Typesetting by *Blue Friday/Candace Creasy*

10 9 8 7 6 5 4 3 2 1

Chronicle Books LLC
680 Second Street
San Francisco, CA 94107
www.chroniclebooks.com

THIS BOOK IS DEDICATED TO MY GRANDMOTHER ELOISE, OF COURSE;

TO FOUR GOOD FRIENDS WHO HELPED LAUNCH MY URBAN FARMING CAREER: SANDY HEAD, PAUL SCHRADE, SHERRY, AND FRED;

TO THE TIRELESS AND DEVOTED ANGELA RINALDI AND ROB STEINER;

AND TO ANYONE WHO HAS EVER PUT A SEED IN THE GROUND AND WATCHED IT GROW.

ACKNOWLEDGMENTS

We would like to thank the following people, whose generous help, input, and, in many cases, shared gardens made this book possible.

Andrew Beckman; Judith Belzer; Jonathan Berg; Mort Bernstein; Michelle Clair; Robin and Manny Coto; Nancy Deane; Chloe Rose Elia; Annette Elmo; Sasha Emerson; Jacob Epstein; Elena Esparza; Claire Fletcher; Sarajo Frieden; Kristina Fukuda-Schmid; Dede Gardner-Berg; Laurel Garza; Steve Goto; Grandmother Nana; John, Laura, Marcia, and Michael Heeger; John and Diane Hertz; Gail Hochman; Tim and Julia Johnson; Kiki Kapany; Safa Kasem-Hayes; Jennifer Kell; Kiran; Jeannie Kusserow; Lily Pearl Langos; Jason La Padura; Josh Loeb; Christina Loff; Thomas McCarry; Susan McKean; Bill McKibben; Echo, Fin, and Tato Miyamoto; Patricia Moritz; Gary Murphy; Zoe Nathan; Susie Norris; Michael Pollan; Michelle Reiner; Nicole Rouzan; Martha Ryan; Jessica Sanchez; Yvonne Savio; Andrew Schapiro; Michael Schwarz; Bill Shank; Laurie Sorenson; Naomi Starkman; Hannah, Otto, and Saida Staudenmaier; Simon Steiner; Alexandra, Dominic, Luc, and Zita Surprenant; Amy Treadwell; Jodi Warshaw; Monica Weil; Brody, Derrick, Elaine, Fred, Gary, Gertrude, Larry, Lawrence, Logan, Patrice, Porter, Rosanne, Terry, Thelma, and Wayne Williams; and Richie Wingfield.

TABLE OF CONTENTS

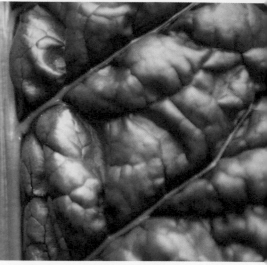

FOREWORD

BILL MCKIBBEN,

AUTHOR *Earth: Making a Life on a Tough New Planet*

There are a number of stories that people endlessly repeat about local food, and indeed, about anything environmentally sane: that it's for rich people, that it's for white people, that it's just some trendy lifestyle. This beautiful book sets the lie to those notions. The author's great-great-great-grandmother brought tomato seeds in her apron pocket on a slave ship—he grew up eating the descendants of those 'Goosecreek' tomatoes with his eleven siblings in their Long Island, New York, home, and it was the first variety he grew to sell in the farmers' markets of Los Angeles. It's the kind of story that reminds us that most people on this planet are unconsciously environmental—and that those good habits lie buried, dormant in us, like seeds waiting for the spring rain.

But of course good intentions are not enough, so the next best thing about this volume is the fact that it simply and straightforwardly demystifies vegetable gardening. You don't need immense amounts of equipment, or space, or expertise to get started—but it will help enormously to have these simple suggestions, diagrams, and photos to inspire and illuminate.

Don't read it if you want an excuse not to garden—by the time you're done, you won't have any.

Finally, it reminds us that food really is the place to start—not just to make environmental sense but to build community, which is, in the end, even more important. One of my favorite statistics: The average shopper at a farmers' market has ten times more conversations per visit than the average shopper at a supermarket. They're having the kind of conversations you'll find in these pages—lively, joyful, informed. This is a passport to a different world—one that much of the planet inhabits, and that you can too.

I was raised in a family of twelve children in African-American neighborhoods around Eastern Long Island, and for us, growing food was a necessity. We had to work in the garden if we wanted to eat. But for me, gardening quickly moved beyond work to something much more intriguing and absorbing. Watching my grandmother Eloise—my first gardening teacher—tend her plants made them interesting. It opened up a world to me—a small universe of complex, interconnected lives that I could be a part of.

MIRACLES IN DRESSER DRAWERS

My grandmother—a South Carolina native who grew up in a traditional Gullah community whose members were descendants of Caribbean slaves—learned to garden from *her* grandmother. She had a confident touch with plants, very focused and deliberate. She wasted nothing—food, words, even her own energy. Funny, wise, and patient, she taught us by example to value what we could make with our hands. For her, cast-off dresser drawers, divided into compartments, made perfect trays for growing seedlings, and every day, she and I would go out first thing to check on these, watching for signs of germination. Though all of us children gardened, I was my grandmother's special helper, the one who took to it most and didn't see it as a chore.

I loved spotting the first tiny green shoots and, a short time later, helping her choose the strongest, most vigorous seedlings to plant out in the garden. The weaker seedlings, those not up to her strict standards, I would toss, along with our kitchen scraps, on an open-pit compost pile behind the house, where growing things got a second chance. This pile, in turn, made the fuel for our garden's annual, magical rebirth. When spring arrived, I couldn't wait to pull the boards off the pit and feel the promising intensity of its heat.

OBSESSED, AGAIN

Germination, compost, and the living bounty of soil continued to intrigue me. Ten years ago, the pull of the soil led me to sideline my first career as a successful sportswear designer (for Calvin Klein, Cacharel, and Anne Cole, and then for my own line, Jimmy Williams Stitches) to go into growing full time. I dug up my Los Angeles yard and obsessively planted every available space in edibles: collard greens, chile peppers, pole beans, tomatoes, melons, and squash. Even the roof of my garage was fair game: It became my growing ground for heirloom seedlings.

By word of mouth, my little enterprise grew. People began showing up for my informal Saturday seedling sales and then asking me if I would build *their* vegetable gardens to accommodate all the plants they bought.

So many of my grandmother's gardening practices serve me today and at least partly account for my own thriving business as a Los Angeles urban farmer and garden designer. Applying what I learned from Eloise, I continue to raise my own heirloom vegetable and herb seedlings, which I sell through the Hollywood and Santa Monica farmers' markets, and my company, HayGround Organic Gardening. Through the same

Chloe Rose Elia, one of my young farmers' market customers, picks out herbs.

Susan and I talk tomatoes over a basket of the 'Goosecreek' variety my family has grown for generations.

company (named for the old Native American practice of covering edible beds with hay for winter), I design and plant vegetable gardens for clients around the city, including some of the region's best-known chefs. For me, there's still a deep magic in a proper soil mix and a miracle in a ripe tomato—its juicy heart, its smell, and, of course, its taste.

FINDING SUSAN

Susan Heeger, a friend and former staff writer for *Martha Stewart Living,* shares my enthusiasm for the idea that cooking simple meals with what you grow is an almost indescribable pleasure—but so is growing it in the first place. She believes, as I do, that digging the soil is a fundamental satisfaction for a human being, and one that counteracts life's trials and stresses. We met in 2001, after *Garden Design* magazine ran a story on me and my garden. A well-known Los Angeles feature writer (who co-wrote *The Gardens of California* with landscape designer Nancy Goslee Power), Susan came to interview me for a *Los Angeles Times* magazine article. Her stories brought more attention to me and my business and sparked others—among them, pieces in *Cottage Living, Los Angeles, Food & Wine,* and various television feature segments.

It was the beginning of our friendship. As a dedicated vegetable gardener in her own right, Susan has watched with me

as enthusiasm for edible gardening has surged on the national level. This has happened partly in response to the writings of journalists like Michael Pollan, who has encouraged us to rethink how and what we eat; the birth of organizations like Kitchen Gardens International, dedicated to home food growing; and the efforts of activists such as Fritz Haeg, who encourages homeowners to swap their front lawns for vegetable crops.

But amid this rising interest, Susan and I have also noticed a lack of available resource books for people trying to grow their own food and grow it right, which was always my grandmother's aim. "I may not be the best gardener, but I'm the best gardener I know," she used to say, smiling in her sun hat.

THE IDEA GROWS

As Eloise's gardening grandson, I have been carrying around an idea for years, one that sprouted from the seeds of her wisdom, and also, really, from the seeds of a tomato *her* great-grandmother brought to South Carolina on a slave ship, in her apron pocket. That 'Goosecreek' tomato, which I grew up eating around a wooden table with my family, was the first variety I grew to sell and the one that first sold my early customers on me. Buying it and tasting it, they came back and bought other seedlings from me. Along with asking me how to grow

NOTHING IS MORE LOCAL AND FRESH AND TASTES BETTER THAN WHAT YOU GROW YOURSELF.

these things, they began asking me what I do with them in the kitchen—what *I* cook with what *I* pick.

And, of course, my answers owe a lot to my grandma Eloise—the Gullah food traditions of South Carolina—and to my other grandmother, Muriel ("Nana"), who was half Shinnecock Indian and cooked the corn cakes and succotash of *that* cuisine. My mother played her part in distilling these traditions, when, out of necessity, she and Eloise taught us twelve kids to cook, with love and humor, in our own big, country-style kitchen.

From Seed to Skillet is rooted in a bygone time when kitchen gardening was widespread, but it belongs to the current era, as more and more people discover the satisfaction of growing their own food.

LISTENING TO VEGETABLES

Decades ago, certainly during World Wars I and II, kitchen gardens were considered necessary—and patriotic. Back then, Americans consulted family elders for growing tips and swapped seeds with their neighbors. Every vegetable had a story—beginning with some dedicated seed saver, perhaps a trip in a smuggler's trunk across a border, maybe a father-to-son pact to preserve a cultural taste or tradition. The wisdom of the earth wasn't an obscure or arcane science reserved for the few, but an everyday, natural part of life, and survival.

Obviously, for many years, that wisdom fell by the wayside for most of us. Too busy to garden and happy for the miracle of supermarkets, we lost touch with the source of our food. We didn't think about the cost to our country of the emergence of industrial farming, the elimination of crop diversity in favor of efficiency and profit, or the damage to the planet when food is shipped vast distances from where it's grown.

Yet all that is changing fast. In 2005, four California women declared themselves "locavores" and made a month's commitment to eat only food produced within one hundred miles of their homes. Their effort got so much attention that others followed their lead, and the *New Oxford American Dictionary* named "locavore" its 2007 word of the year. Right now, as food and fuel prices climb to all-time highs, fresh, local produce is especially in demand. In fact, it's the second-biggest American food trend. Just as significant, as the *New York Times* and *Wall Street Journal* have lately reported, Americans are buying great quantities of vegetable seeds and seedlings to grow themselves. Because nothing is more local and fresh and tastes better than what you grow yourself.

MAKING IT HAPPEN

With household vegetable gardening on the rise, *From Seed to Skillet* is a comprehensive guide to choosing, planting, tending, harvesting, and using homegrown organic vegetables.

It presents a way to live richly—by closely linking the enjoyment of home growing with the pleasures of simple home cooking.

This book focuses on a list of food must-haves, and my recommendations for the best heirloom varieties. By choosing heirlooms—storied varieties that have been around for more than half a century—gardeners not only ensure the preservation of our complex food heritage, they also produce prettier and more varied vegetables (striped tomatoes, white eggplants), from which they can save seed and grow more. What they pick will be beautiful and healthy. The vegetables will taste alive and amazing.

It's fascinating to me how different food traditions have grown up around the same plants in far-flung places. Think, for instance, of the tomato's central role in the cuisines of Italy and Mexico, and you might conclude, as I have, that food offers a bridge among cultures, a way for people to understand each other. What's more, when you know where a plant is from and where it's traveled to, you have a window on its character—and a leg up on growing it better.

Then, of course, there are health benefits that enhance the pleasures of edible gardening. True, not everyone has the acre parcel my grandmother had for growing, so this book will present different options for cultivating crops—in the strip of ground behind a garage, in a couple of raised beds outside the kitchen, and even in a few pots along a sunny driveway. To demonstrate the possibilities, we will give you examples, with pictures, from my clients' gardens and from Susan's and my own.

Next, we will lay out crucial steps in the planning and preparation process: where to look for good seeds and seedlings; how to assemble the right tools and soil components; and how to ready beds and select good growing companions, including beneficial flowers. If you understand soil basics, it's a snap to make it produce, as people have done for thousands of years. Whether gardeners start small, with one basil pot, or turn their front lawn into a farm, the growing process is the same. Good soil is the secret, and Susan and I will show you how to make it. We will present some of my most effective recipes for feeding the soil, and by extension, the vegetables themselves.

SECRETS FOR SUCCESS

Tending tips will follow too—compost and watering advice, along with prescriptions for reducing pests and boosting production. We will cover harvesting and seed saving, which enables gardeners to replant top performers. We will also discuss the basics of crop rotation, ensuring fertile soil and ample yields year after year.

Finally, we will offer delicious possibilities from the Williams kitchen—easy recipes for transforming the fresh bounty from the garden into something luscious for the table. When you cook what you have grown, you come full-circle, completing a timeless and deeply satisfying act that begins with the magic of a seed.

CHAPTER

1

THE SEEDS OF MY GARDENING SOUL

Most gardeners have a story that explains how they got hooked on growing things. It might revolve around a taste—a bite of a berry from a neighbor's yard—or a memory of home, such as the urge to re-create a beloved mother's potato plot. It could turn on serendipity; renting a house, say, that comes with an herb garden, which you discover you love to tend. In my case, the story isn't simple or straightforward. I started gardening, as I have said, from necessity, and my mentor became a role model for my life. So much of what I do now seems to have been preordained from my childhood world, and that world was dominated by Eloise.

No experience is needed to tend the mixed lettuce baskets I offer at the farmers' market.

TO BE *SOMEBODY*

My grandmother Eloise was an expert at organizing children to do what needed doing. "You—go get the shovel," she would say to me or one of my brothers. "And you—" to one of my sisters, "I need the wheelbarrow and the rake." In her house-dress and apron, the straw hat low on her head, she worked right along with us, hoeing weeds and spreading compost. With seventeen grown children of her own, she folded the oldest of us Williams kids into her household for several years—the years my father, her son Lawrence, was in the Army and away from home. When he came back, he and my mother Gertrude bought a house down the street from Eloise, which gave us more time in her character-building orbit.

A small, plump, lively woman with gray braids and a ringing voice, Eloise was a widow, having lost her husband years before to a reckless driver on a country road. "Weezy," we called her lovingly—behind her back. To her face she was always Grandma, the strict, somewhat formal product of her Gullah raising. Gullah people tend toward the self-reliant and the clannish. Said to be the closest African-Americans to their African home cultures, they even have their own language, a kind of African-English that's hard for outsiders to understand.

On Long Island, where, via Philadelphia, she had arrived as a young woman, Eloise was herself a bit of an outsider. She never warmed completely to my mother, who, with her Shinnecock Indian and Irish blood, was lighter-skinned, with reddish hair—traits that didn't matter to Gertrude but that made Eloise uncomfortable. Also, Gertrude was Catholic, and Eloise was an enthusiastic, "foot-stomping" Baptist. Outside church, though, she was more reserved, while Gertrude was the kind of big-hearted mother who gathered stray children from the neighborhood and sat them down at our table.

But Gertrude and Eloise understood and trusted each other. For a while, they shared the job of raising us. Eloise

[ELOISE] HARANGUED US TO "BE SOMEBODY," TO STRIVE TO ACCOMPLISH THINGS WITH NO HELP FROM ANYONE ELSE.

My son, Logan, and nursery assistant Jessica Sanchez get a lesson in seed planting.

took us to church. With my mother's approval, she preached at us about hard work, self-respect, practicing our best manners. She harangued us to "be somebody," to strive to accomplish things with no help from anyone else. "Play in your own yard," she would say, with snappy Gullah pride.

THE BEAUTY OF ORDER

Twice a year, Eloise took the train back to South Carolina as if to remind herself of who she was. She always came back with seeds—for 'Goosecreek' tomatoes, 'Cowhorn' okra, sweet

potatoes, and peppers that she would swap with neighbor women for Long Island corn, onion, and potato seeds. These she stored in neatly labeled glass jars on shelves in her garden shed, and they gave her the greatest pleasure. In the jewel-like corn kernels and speckled butterbeans, in the small dots of hot peppers, she saw the promise of the future. I saw it too, like coins, like money in the bank, waiting to be transformed into food.

This was the yearly miracle that we children took part in. As if by magic, Eloise brought the promise of her jars to life, in a garden made to be practical more than pretty, but that—to me—was both. A ripple of rhubarb ran down one side, a bed of cutting flowers across the back. In May, her tidy patchwork showed only faint, greening stripes along the ground, but

FROM SEED TO SKILLET

CHILDREN DON'T GET MUCH CHANCE TO FEEL POWERFUL IN THE WORLD. IN THE GARDEN, I WAS SUDDENLY PART OF SOMETHING BIGGER THAN MYSELF, SOMETHING COLORFUL AND ALIVE THAT SHOWED ME THE POTENTIALLY DRAMATIC IMPACT OF MY ACTIONS.

In my growing grounds (above), I tend the seedlings till they're big enough for Logan and me to take to market (below, right).

by July, the plants were big enough to tussle, with top-heavy tomatoes straining at their ties and squash and melons jostling to engulf the earth.

Watching Eloise work—and carrying out her endless orders—I learned to do what she could do. Not that she explained herself. She taught us by example, filling her seed trays with potting soil she'd mixed with peat moss, tucking the seeds in carefully, setting the trays in a protected spot where she could watch for marauding birds that would steal the seeds from a garden bed. She planted seedlings to give her plants a better start. And this allowed her to grow the best of them, which she let me help her pick. The power of the task excited me. As I looked over leaves and tested stems for sturdiness, I thought to myself, "You, but not you; you, but not you," feeling oh-so-lordly.

A BIGGER PICTURE

This is what sold me very early on gardening, as opposed to my other chores. Children don't get much chance to feel powerful in the world. In the garden, I was suddenly part of something bigger than myself, something colorful and alive that showed me the potentially dramatic impact of my actions. Because of things I did, plants were born, grew, fed us, and died. They left something behind, though, something that re-ignited the process. Eloise taught me how to help this happen, how to squeeze the pulp from a tomato into a bucket, add an inch of water, then put the bucket in the shade until it formed a smelly white fungus. It was time then to strain and wash the seeds and wrap them in paper away from the sun. When they were dry, they were viable: They would produce exactly the same tomatoes they had come from, a quality of heirloom seeds that isn't true of their hybrid cousins. With hybrids, which are a mix of many plant strains, you don't know what you'll get when you replant the seeds—something I didn't learn until much later.

Nor did I know then why compost is a better plant food than the chemical fertilizers nurseries sell. As a child, I didn't know there *were* such things as chemical fertilizers, and they didn't register much for Eloise either. There was a spring ritual in her garden, and in our own garden down the street, of uncovering compost that had simmered in the ground all winter. When we stuck a shovel in it, worms wiggled out. It was rich and crumbly and smelled sweet. When we dug it

into garden beds, or when we steeped it in water, strained it, and sprayed it on leaves, our plants grew strong and stout. Chewing bugs stayed away. Our vegetables were all but perfect.

THE ONGOING CYCLE

In the fall, once we'd picked the garden clean, we yanked out the plants in a kind of ritualistic slaughter and pitched *them* on the compost pile, there to cook, under cover, through the cold. Everything had its season; nothing went to waste. In fact, the summer's bounty fed us through the winter—from kitchen shelves filled with string beans, peppers, onions, carrots, tomatoes, and peaches preserved in more of Eloise's jars.

Though on some level this was all routine work for her, I felt Eloise's deep satisfaction in growing things, and then in cooking what she'd grown into foods she'd grown up eating. I'm sure it helped her to feel connected to home—not only to recreate her childhood foods but to teach my mother (who wanted to please my father) how to cook them too.

Both women loved to cook, and for both, cooking was synonymous with affection and tradition. My mother's lima bean soup honored *her* mother, our Nana, and transmitted Nana's kindness to us. Eloise's Gullah rice dishes, like the seeds her family had saved, were another part of our inheritance, and our mother cherished and preserved them too.

FOOD AND FAMILY

To this day, when I smell rice—especially rice that has been browned some before cooking and spiked with fresh-chopped okra, green peppers, or tangy kale—I think of Eloise at her enormous coal-fed stove, and Gertrude at hers. I remember dinners around their tables, some of us sitting and eating, passing big clay bowls and plates of cornbread, some of us standing, waiting to claim vacated chairs, everyone talking about the day, enjoying each other's company.

Food brings people together in happy ways, and something magical happens when the food you eat is the product of your labor. The pleasure intensifies when the whole family has played a part.

Luc Surprenant, another young client, helps with the harvest in his Malibu garden.

Kristina Fukuda-Schmid (above) shops for summer plants in Santa Monica, where my June selection includes (below, left to right) basil, tomatoes, 'Golden Muscat' grapes, and peppers.

FOOD BRINGS PEOPLE TOGETHER IN HAPPY WAYS, AND SOMETHING MAGICAL HAPPENS WHEN THE FOOD YOU EAT IS THE PRODUCT OF YOUR LABOR.

Amaranth (above). Debating herbs with Jason La Padura and Gary Murphy (above, right). Lemon thyme (below, left).
Cat grass and assorted basils (below, right).

SMALL CHILDREN ARE MORE INCLINED TO EAT A VEGETABLE THEY PICK THAN ONE THAT ARRIVES, FROM PARTS UNKNOWN, TO FILL THEIR PLATES.

A GROWING OBSESSION

In my business, through the years, I have started small with many of my farmers' market customers, selling them only a plant or two with instructions for container growing on a terrace. For a lot of them, one low-key success has sparked a fire: Picking their first tomato—which they've planted, watered, and tended themselves—they're already looking around for more ground to co-opt, driveways and flower beds to turn into more edibles. It doesn't, they realize, require much money. It isn't difficult to do. And when you understand your plants' needs, it only gets easier. More and more, as you progress, what's for dinner in your house depends on what's ripe for picking outside.

It's an oddly addictive process. When I lived in New York and was still designing clothes, I used to take the Long Island Railroad to my parents' house on weekends, just to tend my mother's vegetables. I looked for books on edible gardening; I read everything I could find, building on my grandma's wisdom with information on the chemistry of soil and the principles of organic pest control. Even before I left New York, I installed my first garden for a non-family member on a Manhattan rooftop—because I *had* to plant something somewhere.

Small children immediately understand the thrill of plunging their hands into dirt. They're also more inclined to eat a vegetable they pick than one that arrives, from parts unknown, to fill their plates. My two children grew up helping me in my Los Angeles garden, and many of my customers have had the same bonding experience with their kids. Gardening, more than anything else I know, teaches patience, generosity, and sharing. It makes us partners with nature and illuminates the cycles of the seasons.

A BOY AND HIS CROPS

Recently, one of my clients called me and put her five-year-old son on the phone with some questions about tomatoes. What color were they when they got ripe? How did you know when to pick them? Remembering him from one of the farmers' markets, I asked him to remind me which of my tomatoes he and his mother had bought. Prompted by her cues from the background, he told me 'Brown Berry', 'St. Pierre', and 'Mango'. I said, "Brownish-red, bright red, and orange," answers he had to dictate to his mom, since he couldn't write. His voice quivered with excitement. Before the call ended, he was already running out to check the crops. "He's obsessed," his mother told me.

I share his obsession. I'm every bit as excited. I know that with a little more information, clouds part, doubts lift, and you can plunge ahead into an old-fashioned and contemporary process that's as natural as breathing. From a bowl of herbs on a windowsill to my little man's tomato patch, growing food is a primal satisfaction available to all of us. My mission is to help you start, if you haven't already, or to be more successful if you have.

A mix of herbs, greens, and lettuces soak up the sun in my growing grounds.

CHAPTER

2

⟨ OPTIONS FOR GROWING ⟩

As you flip through this book, maybe in a store or a friend's kitchen, you might think that fresh vegetables are all well and good, and you support the concept of eating locally, but for you, growing food is not an option. You have no space—because you rent, or own a condo, or because your garden is already full of ornamental plants. Possibly, time is the issue. Your life is so packed with obligations that you can't take on one more. Or you see yourself as inept at gardening: All your past attempts have been failures. This chapter is for you. Here is where I encourage you to keep reading by showing you that whatever your situation, you too can grow food, if only in a deep pot or window box. I'll help you size up your choices and decide which of many options will get you started on a path that might just change the way you live.

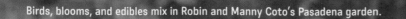
Birds, blooms, and edibles mix in Robin and Manny Coto's Pasadena garden.

The Cotos' garden expresses what they love.

LESSONS FROM THE PAST

It's my belief that there's something in the air right now, something, despite all our attempts to be practical and efficient—our inability to go anywhere without a cell phone or the Internet—that's calling us back to simpler times. They're times many of us easily remember—when people were less dependent on shopping malls and more attuned to their neighbors. When borrowing a cup of sugar or a handful of bean seeds was a common and friendly act. When our grandparents lived with the family, or at least close by, and had lots to do with our proper raising.

While I'm not someone who idealizes the past, I honor its gifts and try to keep them alive with my own children. And more and more, I find I'm not alone.

Traditionally, homegrown food has played a big role for Americans in times of need. In 1917, just before the United States entered World War I, a group called the National War Garden Commission launched an effort to get able-bodied citizens to plant "war gardens," and thereby increase the food supply. If families grew enough to feed themselves, the logic went, then commercial supplies (dwindling drastically as farmers left their farms to fight) would be freed up for our troops.

The same thing happened during the Second World War. A 1942 pamphlet on Victory Gardens, issued by the U.S. Department of Agriculture, urged all Americans to consider it "a public duty, as well as a private necessity," to raise at least some of their household's food. Again, since so much produce was being funneled to soldiers, civilians *needed* gardens to meet their own nutritional requirements. In fact, the booklet

WHILE I'M NOT SOMEONE WHO IDEALIZES THE PAST, I HONOR ITS GIFTS AND TRY TO KEEP THEM ALIVE WITH MY OWN CHILDREN.

went on to say, so many amateur gardeners responded to the call that as early as 1939, production in home gardens had begun to outstrip food from farms.

The feeling that, I think, is overtaking us again, is a drive to reclaim personal power amid factors we can't control. Writer Verlyn Klinkenborg expressed a similar view in a *New York Times* column several months ago. "Perhaps," he wrote, "this is the moment for another national home gardening movement, a time when the burgeoning taste for local food converges with the desire to cut costs and take control over our own battered economic lives." We may have lost a job, seen our pay cut, watched our savings go south. But there's something we can do to help ourselves—something really pretty simple. By planting food for our family, we can shake off at least some of our dependency on others, and lower our grocery bills in the bargain. That feels good. And it makes us part of a time-honored and satisfying natural cycle. Even more importantly, it makes us part of a community. Gardeners, you will find, are very warm and sharing people.

A NURTURING NETWORK

At the farmers' markets where I sell my seedlings, I constantly see gardeners, who have little else apparently in common, bond over their mutual passion for particular plants. One person will notice what another is buying and just have to comment. Someone else will chime in with a story or suggestion about growing. Before long, as my son, Logan, and I watch, they might be exchanging phone numbers or buying a bag of fertilizer to split three ways.

It's no wonder I love my job. The mere *intent* to grow vegetables makes people happy. After all the hard and sometimes solitary work of raising crops, it's wonderful to see this, and to hand over what I cherish to someone else who will cherish it just as much, and tend it until it produces. When I sell a collard tree or some purple asparagus, and pass on tips on how to grow them, I feel like my buyer's partner, and my buyer's *friend's* partner. I've begun the plant's raising; now *they* will complete the task.

Not that I'm not curious about how they intend to do this. I'm always eager to hear this person or that one say that this is the year they're going to scrap their lawn and plant tomatoes, or swap their flowering shrubs for artichokes. Many people talk to me about the impact of the economy—food prices, gas prices—and explain their urge to conserve precious resources, such as garden water, for plants they can eat, not just admire.

I understand this impulse. It's hard for me to see flowering vines without envisioning grapes, or boxwood hedges without mentally substituting blueberries. So entrenched in me is the joy of bringing these things to life that I feel for people who have the nurturing instinct but deny themselves the fun. Because of space. Because of time.

Lettuce and herbs are simple to grow—even in containers.

WHAT *ARE* A BEGINNER'S BEST BETS? WILL 4-INCH POTS OF THYME AND MINT SURVIVE ON A KITCHEN WINDOWSILL? CAN YOU GROW GOOD PEPPERS ON A BALCONY?

DIGGING IN

In my years of garden consulting and designing, here's something I have found: People almost always have *some* space, even if it's just a driveway, the back steps, an apartment deck, or a sun room with good light. And isn't this true too: Time tends to rather magically multiply when you're doing what you enjoy.

I myself have grown lettuce and tomatoes, among other things, in very temporary spots, with time stolen from my working hours. While these garden efforts weren't ideal, they were thrilling—because they showed me I could have what I wanted, if I adjusted my expectations. With each success, I began adjusting my goals as well. If I could harvest amazing greens from a few pots on a deck, what could I do with real *ground*?

In just this way, gardening can change your life. But only if you want it to.

So. What *are* a beginner's best bets? Will 4-inch pots of thyme and mint survive on a kitchen windowsill? Can you grow good peppers on a balcony?

I hear these questions weekly at the markets, and also from my design clients. The answers often surprise them. Some of the best starters are among the most popular edibles—healthy salad greens, and cooking herbs that add fresh, distinctive flavors to our meals. For both the greens and the herbs, *harvesting* doubles as maintenance. The more you cut, the more they grow. Nor do they mind life in a container.

GREENS-IN-A-BOX

To people hesitant to rush headlong into gardening, I like to recommend a modest start that almost inevitably leads to success. Choose several lettuce seedlings—for instance, 'Sweet Valentine', 'Amish Deer Tongue', 'Schweitzer's Mescher Bibb', and 'Yugoslavian Red Butterhead'—and a roomy (at least one-foot-deep) planter box. Fill it with good-quality potting mix (my favorite, from E.B. Stone Organics, is loaded with nutrients) and tuck the lettuce in tight, a mere couple inches apart. Water well and set in a sunny spot. After a few days, you can begin harvesting the outer leaves of head lettuce (they grow from the center), or, with looser, leaf-type lettuce, you can cut the whole head about an inch from the base; it will sprout again before you know it.

PIQUANT POTS

Arugula, a much-sought-after, peppery-tasting salad green, takes to pot culture beautifully. It's best when young and tender, but with frequent harvests, you can keep it that way longer, postponing the time when it blooms and goes to seed. If it does bloom, you can snip and eat the flowers, a delicious novelty you'd pay dearly for at a gourmet grocer's.

BY PLANTING FOOD FOR OUR FAMILY, WE CAN SHAKE OFF AT LEAST SOME OF OUR DEPENDENCY ON OTHERS, AND LOWER OUR GROCERY BILLS IN THE BARGAIN.

In Jennifer Kell and Dominic Surprenant's garden, vegetables grow in raised beds beside a meadow.

Food and play share space in Kell and Surprenant's Malibu landscape (above).

Peppers ripen amid flowers, strawberries, kale, and chard (above and below).

A 1942 PAMPHLET ON VICTORY GARDENS, ISSUED BY THE U.S. DEPARTMENT OF AGRICULTURE, URGED ALL AMERICANS TO CONSIDER IT "A PUBLIC DUTY, AS WELL AS A PRIVATE NECESSITY," TO RAISE AT LEAST SOME OF THEIR HOUSEHOLD'S FOOD.

Susan and her husband Rob Steiner tend edibles year-round in their Los Angeles courtyard.

A potting table doubles as a spot for rose-arranging in Diane and John Hertz's Malibu garden.

Herbs are just as easy to raise: Give rampant growers, like mint, their own container, and shelter shade lovers such as parsley and dill while showering others with sun. Will they thrive indoors? Not indefinitely, though you can certainly start them from seeds in 4-inch pots on a bright windowsill in your kitchen. Before long, as their roots grow, you will need to pot them up to deeper containers that will be too big for the sill. You must also ensure that indoor temperatures are evenly warm (70 degrees F is ideal) and that plants sit near a southern or western window that gets 4 to 5 daily hours of sun.

With any pots, you have to water often, but be careful not to overdo it, which leads to rot, particularly with herbs. (When I start herb seeds, I water seedling trays with a pump sprayer, to avoid drowning them.) Let pots dry out a bit between waterings—until the soil feels dry about 1 inch down—and feed, starting a month after planting, once a month, with compost tea (see page 99) or fish emulsion. Or, you can use a slow-release organic formula like Biosol (available online), according to product directions.

ON DECK: PEPPERS

Yes, you *can* grow peppers, or even tomatoes, on a balcony—after checking how much weight your deck will hold, and keeping in mind that a very large potted plant can weigh 200 pounds or more. Tomatoes want depth—at least 1½ to 2 feet, which means a 15-gallon container. Peppers need less—a mere foot of depth suits them—and they may actually produce more if you contain them.

My favorite container choice is terra-cotta, but a nice, stout, half-wine or whiskey barrel works well too. Many of my clients, even those with full backyards, have had me start them off with such containers, and once they've seen the results, we have usually moved on to build beds. The first shock of success tends to be visual: People who buy a lot of packaged food, or even produce from the grocery store, aren't prepared for the jewel-like reds and pinks and emerald greens of heirloom lettuce, the delicacy of purple sage or curly basil. Of course, the taste is far superior too, which is truly what hooks my customers.

TALES FROM THE TRENCHES

One man I work for already had a very large garden full of flower borders and roses around a lawn, when a friend of his introduced us. He invited me to his house in Malibu, where the only planting spot left was a steep hill sectioned with landscape ties into odd, wedge-shaped parts. I replaced the thin dirt in these compartments with rich potting soil, and filled them with broccoli raab, Swiss chard, parsley, peas, arugula, and kale. About three weeks later, he called me back

PEOPLE ALMOST ALWAYS HAVE *SOME* SPACE FOR GROWING FOOD, EVEN IF IT'S JUST A DRIVEWAY, THE BACK STEPS, AN APARTMENT DECK, OR A SUN ROOM WITH GOOD LIGHT.

to tour his lush, layered, and utterly transformed slope—and to ask me to carve out another vegetable plot from a portion of his lawn.

Another man showed me the rear half of his sunny driveway—a relic from the 1920s, when cars were narrower than they are today. "I never use this; let's get rid of it," he said. While you should check local regulations before taking such a step, it worked for him. We excised half the paving, leaving enough to park on and constructing raised beds in the empty spot, using the broken concrete pieces, stacked and mortared, to make the bed walls.

Some people appreciate formality in vegetable gardens, which tend toward the wild and sprawling. Susan and her husband Rob Steiner, a landscape architect, replaced a basketball court behind their house with four 5-by-9-foot vegetable beds, separated by gravel paths. The result is a lovely courtyard, enclosed on one side by a hedge, on another by a wall, and on the other sides by their house and studio, which overlook it.

I once designed about a quarter-acre of edible beds on a slope in Palos Verdes, near the ocean, for a woman who loved the look of stacked stone. For another order-loving client, with much more limited ground, I had the bottoms sawed off a dozen large terra cotta pots, filled them with soil, and buried them in rows before planting them with herbs. I have exchanged lawns for beds and, in other cases, ringed lawns with undulating vegetable borders in very informal shapes.

ROSES *AND* TOMATOES

One of my favorite solutions to the no-space, scarce-sun dilemma involved a couple of avid gardeners who didn't want to give up the enormous rose collection behind their house. But still, they longed for edibles, especially juicy red tomatoes. As I walked around, I noticed a sliver of land that I rarely see put to use on urban properties—the side yard. Only about 4 feet wide but at least 30 feet long, it was drenched in some of the lot's best light. It was also hidden from the rest of the garden and therefore didn't have to be pretty.

My crew and I arranged sawhorses down half the length of the space and topped them with 2-by-6 boards. We set deep plastic planter tubs on these, and voilà—an herb garden was born! In the remaining area, the owners grow tomatoes in 15-gallon pots, packed close together. They're some of the best tomatoes I've ever tasted!

Would my grandmother approve? Absolutely. She was all for the practical fix. She loved flowers too, though she never would have given over most of her yard to them. Instead, she used them to beautify the margins of her garden, which was built up in mounded beds edged with stones we dug up as we prepared those beds.

In my mind, her garden is still the one I see as I load the van for the market or head off to a client's house. I see her too, pulling her hat on, and I hear her voice: "Come on now, let's get to it."

Tomatoes and roses in the same yard? Definitely!

CHAPTER

3

PLANNING FOR PLANTING

How far ahead must the food gardener start? How do you decide what to grow; where to put it; and whether to plant seeds, seedlings, or a combination of the two? Should you begin with a sketched plan? Start seeds indoors, if you live in a cold climate? How important is your climate zone to your garden choices, and where can you go for zone-specific gardening information? This chapter will answer these questions, suggest seed and plant sources, and offer advice about timing and locating the garden, as well as different variables to consider along the way.

My new Los Angeles growing grounds.

Tree collard greens.

RARING TO GO

Twenty years ago, when my then-wife (and still good friend), Annette Elmo, and I bought our Los Angeles house, I couldn't wait to get a shovel in the ground. Never mind that our 1920s cottage sat on a tiny (40-by-100-foot) lot, or that the backyard's sunniest spot was covered in concrete and an old incinerator left over from the days when people burned leaves in backyard barrels. *So much for you,* I thought, trucking that trash-burner to a scrap yard. In a state of new-homeowner's glee, I spent a couple of days sledgehammering out the concrete, which I saved to reuse in a front-yard path and retaining wall. Nothing would go to waste in my developing world, and everything, from the parkway along the street to my neighbors' garage walls in back, would become a part of the city farm I saw myself creating.

How sweet that labor was! How exhilarating the feeling! For years, from apartment to apartment, I had carried jars of my grandmother's 'Goosecreek' tomato seeds, her speckled butter beans, her Christmas limas. I had planted a few here and there, in terrace pots, and I had tended them faithfully, but this was different. I had *land* now, and the possibilities seemed endless. A couple of weeks before we closed on the house, I even traveled to my parents' Long Island garden for cuttings of the tree collard greens that had passed down through our family for generations. I knew exactly what I was going to raise—the food of home, redolent of happy times that I wanted our children, Logan, then five, and Porter, three, to grow up knowing. Annette felt the same way. She too, in those early days, returned to *her* parents' garden in South Los Angeles for snips of *their* collard greens—a common and traditional edible in African-American neighborhoods.

Even before I finished stacking concrete, I had seeds started in seedling trays and lengths of redwood put aside for a 6-by-8-foot raised bed. A couple of days later, after digging and turning the hard ground on that sunny backyard site, I built my first bed, with Logan as my helper.

All this came back to me as Susan and I sat down recently to talk about garden planning.

ORGANIZE AND IMPROVISE

This key component of any gardener's to-do list is actually as varied and personal as, well, our personalities themselves. Some of us are natural planners, who organize our lives with maps, schedules, and notes to ourselves. Others are improvisers, who like to be surprised. It seems obvious, but as you start your edible garden, you should approach it in a way that's comfortable for you and fits the time and attention you have. Make sure it suits your style and gives you an outlet for creativity.

Certainly, if you design and build beds, you will be plotting them out, taking measurements, and making sketches. If you're going to plant succession crops—replacing plants that produce and then peter out with others that thrive later in the season—you'll have to plan ahead for those. But some experts advise starting *any* garden with graph paper and a pencil, so you can map your ground precisely and make the most of every inch.

This is especially helpful where space is tight. As you fill in the scaled squares with this much lettuce and that many carrots, you'll be able to gauge in advance the number of seeds and seedlings you need to buy, how much room they'll take, and what to swap into their place once their season is done.

MAKE WAY FOR EGGPLANT

Most of the edibles we grow in home gardens are annuals, which means they stay in the ground for no more than a year, and often much less. Take radishes: They may need a mere 3 to 7 days to germinate from seed and another 25 to 30 to reach pickable size. Once picked, they're gone, making room in the bed for something else. At that point, with a bit of foresight, you can be ready with fresh seedlings—eggplant, perhaps—that you've been growing meanwhile in flats or pots. After working a few handfuls of organic compost and some of my own HayGround fertilizer blend (see page 66 for the recipe) into the soil, settle the eggplant in the former radish patch. Then start flats of your *next* seedlings—turnips, say, or winter squash—so you can plug *them* in when summer wanes.

Even in the coldest climates, an organized gardener can harvest successive waves of produce, each in its own time, from spring through autumn. In Southern California, with its year-round growing climate, we also have a full season of winter edibles, which are more or less the same ones cold-climate gardeners plant in early spring, once their soil is warm enough to work. This group includes greens, peas, radishes, cabbage, and onions. Next, as the weather warms, days lengthen, and early crops wind down (somewhere between April in very mild zones and June in harsher ones), it's time to plant everything we associate with the peak of summer: tomatoes, basil, beans, cucumbers, melons. Some of these—certain tomatoes, for example—will continue producing right on into fall. But many

AS YOU START YOUR EDIBLE GARDEN, YOU SHOULD APPROACH IT IN A WAY THAT'S COMFORTABLE FOR YOU AND FITS THE TIME AND ATTENTION YOU HAVE.

will finish, leaving spaces for one last planting of more greens, beets, and other root vegetables. Twice a year, before the spring crop and the fall crop, I recommend enriching beds, again, with the same HayGround fertilizer blend that I'll discuss in detail in the next chapter, when we talk about soil as a key to productivity.

SIMPLE BEGINNINGS

If you're new to vegetable gardening, you may want to limit your efforts during the first year or two to one glorious season of summer classics. There's nothing wrong with starting slowly, and even deciding, as many of my clients do, that you *only* want to grow food in the warm season, when you have the most outdoor leisure time. Just don't be surprised if, as the summer wanes, you find yourself looking to stretch your edible garden into fall—with such impulsive nursery buys as six-packs of lettuce that appreciate the cooler weather.

Of course, certain plant choices demand more advance planning than others. Some, like hot peppers, seem to take forever (30 to 40 days) to germinate. (Though by soaking your seeds in a bio-stimulant, as we will discuss in the next chapter, you can cut that time in half.) Others, such as asparagus, rhubarb, and raspberries, aren't annuals at all but longer-lived plants that require you to map out more permanent space for them. These will be your garden's constants,

occupying one spot year after year while the beds around them change.

GIVERS, TAKERS, AND KEEPING TRACK

Change is good and, of course, natural in a garden. You may know that it wears out the soil, and encourages pest build-up, to put the same annual edible in the same spot every year. It's less well known that some plant choices actually *prepare* the ground for others. I'll say more on this in Chapters 5 and 8, but I mention it now as it relates to garden planning: Peas, for instance (or any legume), enrich soil with nitrogen that the next crop can use. This is why it's good to follow a planting of peas with things like nitrogen-loving corn, carrots, herbs, kale, or heat-tolerant lettuce and *not* tomatoes, peppers, or eggplant, which don't cotton to a lot of nitrogen.

There are also plants with qualities that make them perfect bedmates for others. Garlic deters Japanese beetles from eating nearby raspberry plants; borage discourages worms that prey on tomatoes.

It might be obvious about now that if you keep good notes on what you plant where and how each crop fares, replanting and rotating will be a cinch. Detailed notes are also the way you learn from your mistakes. When something goes wrong— draws bugs, produces little food or none at all—you can look

An arbor twined with morning glory vines marks the entrance to John and Diane Hertz's rose-and-vegetable garden.

SOME OF US ARE NATURAL PLANNERS, WHO ORGANIZE OUR LIVES WITH MAPS, SCHEDULES, AND NOTES TO OURSELVES. OTHERS ARE IMPROVISERS, WHO LIKE TO BE SURPRISED.

back on possible causes and make the necessary alterations when you grow it next time.

THE LEFT-HANDED APPROACH

As I have said, though, we all go about our planning differently. I myself, I must admit, am not entirely the methodical type. A kind of "left-handed" gardener, I'd rather leave room for happy accidents than try to micro-manage all the possibilities. My style is informal. I'm not comfortable with a strict planting grid, at least for myself. Instead, in my own garden, I started with one thing and rambled on from there, giving nature a starring role in the design. I do like surprises, and I don't get discouraged by failure. If a plant doesn't grow for me, I take that as a challenge to try again, under different conditions.

So in place of a backyard plan per se, I built the biggest possible bed in my sunniest spot, since sun is key for most edibles. I made my bed eighteen inches high so I could fill it with great soil that would drain quickly, and I framed it with paths so I could get to it from all sides. In the middle, I constructed a simple willow teepee for cukes to climb, because it's pretty *and* efficient to grow vining plants vertically. Around these, I arranged what my family and I wanted to eat, all in the form of seedlings I had grown from seed. (For me, this is the most important part of planning—working ahead to order

and pot up seeds so they'll grow into seedlings by the time you're ready to plant.)

I rowed out lettuce and other greens along my garden's northern edge, which got some shade from my garage. Eggplant went in close to these, with peppers—both sweet and hot—along the sunny southern edge, and strawberries cascading from all four corners. Finally, to take advantage of my neighbor's south-facing garage wall, I built a second bed, narrower and longer than the first, where I could coax tomatoes—interplanted with pole and runner beans—up the building, and in that way, extend their growing season with borrowed warmth from the wall.

Inspired by how my crops took off, I was soon adding another raised bed and then another, nibbling into a scrubby, unused lawn and moving plants around as I zeroed in on their needs. Some of this very specific cultivation knowledge I had forgotten since childhood, when gardening was a natural part of my daily life. In my L.A. garden, I tended to take notes *after* I had planted and tended awhile—when I saw, for example, that eggplants needed more sun than I had given them (my first crop didn't produce much in its overly sheltered spot) and hot peppers wanted more shade (despite their name, they don't love full southern sun). Some plants, like broccoli, shoot up tall and leafy, looming over shorter companions and stealing their sun. Squash rambles out sideways, snatching turf from *its* mates, unless you give it lots of room, or something to climb on.

And as I claimed more and more ground for edibles, I looked for more space for starting seedlings. That was when I commandeered my garage roof, climbing up there on a ladder

One of a food gardener's most useful tools is a sturdy wheelbarrow.

Just as my grandmother used to do with beets and other hard-hulled seeds, I prepare them for planting by crushing them (between sheets of waxed paper) with a rolling pin. They sprout in half the time they would otherwise.

and rigging up rudimentary tables, complete with netting to keep out seed-eating birds. (Any gaps in the netting and the birds rushed in for a feast—which supported my grandmother's unshakeable faith in starting seeds in protected trays rather than direct-sowing them in a garden bed.)

CONSIDER YOUR CLIMATE

If this sounds a little *too* loose and improvisational, remember that I live in Southern California, where the climate is prime for growing vegetables. It's hard to go terribly wrong here.

We don't have freezing weather to contend with or, at least in my urban neck of the woods, deer, rabbits, or other feeding creatures. And if I wanted to seize the whole yard for food (which, eventually, I just about did), I wasn't left staring at bare dirt come December. By then, my cool-season crops were filling in.

Of course, most American gardeners face far different conditions—and a wide range of them at that. If you live in the snowy north, it makes sense to spend much of your winter planning, and for many gardeners, that's half the fun: dreaming over catalogs, making lists, anticipating spring. Some cold-climate gardeners order their seeds in late fall and start them in greenhouses or cold frames (transparent mini-shelters you can set right into your beds), or on heated pads under grow lights indoors. They read seed packets carefully, calculating ahead how many weeks each seed type needs for germination and growth. The minute it's planting time, they have seedlings ready to go.

Others in cool zones mail-order cold-hardy seedling varieties. (Many of my recommended seed sources, listed at the end of this chapter, also sell seedlings.) Or they buy them locally, as soon as they can find them in nurseries. 'Alaska' peas, for instance, can go in the ground once the soil is diggable, and they won't suffer if a late frost hits.

up at last. Outside, it would be cold and snowy, the trees bare, the world wintery. But inside, in the bright shelter of the sun porch, *life* was stirring, and that got us so excited, we checked its progress every day. Soon, even before the weather warmed, Eloise would give us the signal that it was time to start putting our plants outside in the sun, both to give them more light and to acclimate them to the cooler temperatures outdoors. That way, if frost struck once we'd planted them in the garden, they survived.

STARTING SEEDS WITH ELOISE

I can trace my own enthusiasm for seed-starting back to my grandmother's house, where we always went the seed route. She directed us with military precision, beginning two months before the last frost generally hit our part of Long Island. A big glassed-in sun porch was the heart of her operation, with a windowed garage to handle the overflow. In both these spots—on the floor, on benches, on tables—we sowed our seeds in cut-up milk cartons, cast-off nursery flats, and (my favorite) bureau drawers partitioned with newspaper or wooden sticks. It was the job of us children to fill these containers with potting soil in preparation for the first round of spring crops.

These early peas, beets, cabbage, and greens didn't mind, and even preferred, the lingering cold of winter, and they were our garden's first fresh spring foods. For that reason alone, we were especially thrilled by them: Like us, after the slow quiet of the cold months, they were raring to burst out of their confinement. Naturally, we loved the bounty of summer too, particularly sun-warmed tomatoes and melons. For different reasons, we looked forward to each garden transition, during which we dutifully prepared the soil by feeding it with more compost.

Some of our early-crop seeds (beets and chard, most notably) had hard shells that needed prepping before sowing. My grandmother—who, to me, understood all the deep, locked-in secrets of plants—would fold these between sheets of waxed paper and press them with a rolling pin to crack their hulls. (They sprouted in half the time.)

The others we simply pushed into soil-filled trays, setting them in our sunny windows to germinate, which typically took between 1 and 3 weeks. I remember watching closely for the first green sprouts, the tiny curled stems that reached up and stretched like little sleepers, happy, I always thought, to get

PLANT BY NUMBERS

Of course, it's different for me now. I raise seedlings outside year-round, and that took some getting used to. In fact, wherever you live, it's important to understand your climate. A great resource for help is your closest branch of the Cooperative Extension Service Office. This national network, sponsored by the U.S. Department of Agriculture (USDA), has experts throughout the country who provide region-specific advice to farmers, students, and just-plain people with questions on garden-related issues. They'll help you identify your numbered USDA climate zone, a key factor in determining what you can and can't grow, as well as navigating garden books and catalogs, where information is often zone-specific (you can find your zone online, too, at the U.S. National Arboretum's USDA Plant Hardiness Zone map, at usna.usda.gov/Hardzone/ushzmap.html).

But even more crucial when you're growing vegetables is to know your region's average last frost date in spring and first frost date in fall. These dates bookend your growing season and tell you roughly how many days you have to work with. Knowing this, you can choose plant varieties accordingly.

If you live in Zone 3, for example, where the warm season is very short, you would opt to grow an early-ripening tomato (say, 'Sophie's Choice' or 'Stupice'), rather than one (like big 'Yellow Brandywine') that matures late, when your garden might be getting icy. Again, your closest Cooperative Extension Service Office or a nearby garden supply store will be able to give you the information.

True, once you know the parameters, you can always try pushing your luck with something you dearly want to grow. Experimenting adds to the thrill of gardening, as long as you balance experiments with a majority of sensible picks. Maybe *this* year, you'll have an extra-warm, extra-long summer and

FOR YEARS, FROM APARTMENT TO APARTMENT, I HAD CARRIED JARS OF MY GRANDMOTHER'S 'GOOSECREEK' TOMATO SEEDS, HER SPECKLED BUTTER BEANS, HER CHRISTMAS LIMAS.

MOST OF THE EDIBLES WE GROW IN HOME GARDENS ARE ANNUALS, WHICH MEANS THEY STAY IN THE GROUND FOR NO MORE THAN A YEAR, AND OFTEN MUCH LESS.

The beauty of food plants, including strawberries (above, left); beans (above, right); and lemons (below, left) adds immeasurably to outdoor living spots.

your one 'Yellow Brandywine' *will* produce. If not, though, with good planning, you will have planted enough early tomatoes that you won't feel too deprived.

LAYING THE FOUNDATIONS

Wherever you live, if you've never grown vegetables before, start small and keep it simple. Try to locate your garden near a water source and your kitchen (the closer it is, the more you'll cook from it), but definitely where there's maximum sun. One of my clients, who lives in a eucalyptus-shaded canyon, had me plant his edibles along the street, which is the brightest spot on his lot. For another client, whose only sun hits a backyard deck, I designed deep, long planting boxes to tuck behind benches, so the back of each bench doubles as a wall of a box.

All my gardens begin with a conversation about tastes. "Let's grow things you love to eat," I always tell people, because that guarantees they will use the harvest, feel inspired, and want to keep on with their growing. So many of us remember old-fashioned, fresh-picked tomatoes—in contrast to their dry, tasteless supermarket kin—that this is the top crop people request. Lettuce, peppers, and herbs come next, but your choices are limited only, really, by your imagination and, if you want to stretch beyond the summer season, your willingness to plan ahead.

Starting plants from seeds gives you the widest range of options and costs less than buying seedlings (which makes sense, since you're doing all the work yourself). Many gardeners, of course, prefer seedlings for their convenience. They're also handy if you start gardening a bit late in the season and can't wait for seeds to sprout. My advice is, try both. Seeds may be more demanding, but you can often find more unusual varieties in seed form. Then, when you sow them in flats, you can select the strongest and best to grow on into plants, throwing the rest on the compost or in a salad.

Some seeds—above all, carrots, radishes, and lettuce—germinate so quickly and grow so willingly into strong, prolific plants that they're my chief exceptions to the rule against direct sowing. You needn't raise them first in flats or pots but instead, you can plant these seeds (following packet directions) directly in your spring garden bed, thinning them as they sprout (again, following packet directions about spacing). I promise, it's a miracle each time the first little shoots appear.

WHERE TO LOOK

Happily, for all of us, the Internet teems with great seed and seedling sources that open up a world of options to the adventurous gardener. Along with rare and storied varieties you won't find in nurseries, their Web sites and catalogs offer growing information and often products and equipment that can boost your gardening success. In addition to my favorite sources, listed on the next two pages, I've also mentioned things I especially like them for. But I'd like to put in a plug, too, for farmers' markets, which, during prime spring and summer garden seasons, can also be excellent places to find organic seedlings, and to talk to friendly growers for cultivation tips.

Remember that a "certified organic" or "certified naturally grown" source ensures that you're filling your garden—and your family's table—with food that doesn't contain chemical residues or heavy metals from chemical fertilizers. And heirloom plants, besides having colorful histories, will grow "true" (duplicate themselves) from seed, so if you save some of their seeds, you can plant them, free of charge, again. You might soon be swapping seeds with other gardeners too, a practice common in my grandmother's world and one that added considerably to her social life. No one appreciates you in quite the same way as one with whom you've shared the fruits of your labor, along with your knowledge and experience as the grower.

So without getting too stressed about it, do give yourself time to settle in with some catalogs, make some growing plans, order, and start seeds. The anticipation of what's ahead is all part of the adventure.

TOP SEED AND SEEDLING SOURCES

My own company, HayGround Organic Gardening, is a great source for a wide variety of herb and vegetable seedlings if you live in Los Angeles. But I have come to love the following sources too—for their rare and unusual offerings; their juicy, information-packed catalogs; and their quality customer service. They all have very user-friendly Web sites, full of tips and inspiration for the edible gardener.

BAKER CREEK HEIRLOOM SEEDS

MANSFIELD, MO; 417-924-8917; RARESEEDS.COM

The owner travels far and wide for seed and offers varieties no one else has—old heirloom corn and beets, amazing melons, and even Chinese red noodle beans! The company also sells garlic, onions, and a great selection of tomato seeds, and produces what I consider the best catalog of all!

DIXONDALE FARMS

CARRIZO SPRINGS, TX; 877-367-1015; DIXONDALEFARMS.COM

Their Web site says they're the largest and oldest onion plant farm in the United States, and I believe them! They carry terrific onions and leeks, and the fertilizers to go with them.

FILAREE FARM

OKANOGAN, WA; 509-422-6940; FILAREEFARM.COM

These are the garlic people, par excellence! You order; they send you the bulbs, ready to plant.

GARDENER'S SUPPLY CO.

BURLINGTON, VT; 888-833-1412; GARDENERS.COM

Among the best sources for gardening supplies, accessories, soil boosters, seed-starting equipment, garden pots, and books, this company does sell seeds and plants too, as you'll see in its very useful catalog.

GARDENS ALIVE!

LAWRENCEBURG, IN; 513-354-1482; GARDENSALIVE.COM

These are, in my opinion, the best organic pest-control people in the country. In addition to all sorts of safe pest-control solutions, they sell very good fertilizers, as well as seeds and seedlings.

GURNEY'S SEED & NURSERY CO.

GREENDALE, IN; 513-354-1491; GURNEYS.COM

They carry a wide range of fruit and nut trees, berries, a huge list of vegetable seeds, seedlings, and garden supplies.

HENRY FIELD'S SEED & NURSERY CO.

AURORA, IN; 513-354-1495; HENRYFIELDS.COM

Here, you'll find fruit and nut trees, vegetable seeds and plants, an impressive selection of berries, my favorite purple asparagus, and a good list of growing supplies.

JOHN SCHEEPERS KITCHEN GARDEN SEEDS

BANTAM, CT; 860-567-6086; KITCHENGARDENSEEDS.COM

Look to their irresistible catalog for lots of unusual vegetable seeds, potato tubers, onion sets, and garlic bulbs.

PEACEFUL VALLEY FARM & GARDEN SUPPLY

GRASS VALLEY, CA; 888-784-1722; GROWORGANIC.COM

This company is a treasure; it's a phenomenal source of gardening information, vegetable seeds and plants, wonderful fertilizers and soil boosters, bare-root fruit trees, berries, artichokes, asparagus, rhubarb, and grape vines. They sell to commercial farms as well as individual gardeners, so you can buy bulk quantities of your chosen miracle products.

PINETREE GARDEN SEEDS

NEW GLOUCESTER, ME; 207-926-3400; SUPERSEEDS.COM

Besides a fine, all-around selection of vegetable seeds and a pretty catalog, they offer potato tubers, onion sets, and berry and rhubarb plants.

SEED SAVERS EXCHANGE

DECORAH, IA; 563-382-5990; SEEDSAVERS.ORG

Founded in 1975, this non-profit membership organization saves and shares the heirloom seeds of America's garden heritage. You don't have to be a member to buy from their online catalog, where you can also find tomato, pepper, and ground cherry seedlings. If you *are* a member, as I am, you can swap seeds with other seed saver members, and get a 10 percent discount on any purchases.

SEEDS OF CHANGE

SPICER, MN; 888-762-7333; SEEDSOFCHANGE.COM

Their mission is maintaining the diversity of edibles in the United States. They sell mostly seeds, heirloom and certified organic, as well as tomato, pepper, onion, and herb seedlings.

SOUTHERN EXPOSURE SEED EXCHANGE

MINERAL, VA; 540-894-9480; SOUTHERNEXPOSURE.COM

They encourage seed saving. If you have seed for something they don't have, they'll make an exchange. They too have an incredible catalog, and I especially love their selection of seeds for greens and potatoes.

STARK BRO'S NURSERIES AND ORCHARDS CO.

LOUISIANA, MO; 800-325-4180; STARKBROS.COM

They specialize in fruit and nut trees and berries, selling seeds, seedlings, and bare-root plants. They also carry rhubarb and asparagus.

TERRITORIAL SEED CO.

COTTAGE GROVE, OR; 800-626-0866; TERRITORIALSEED.COM

Great catalog and an impressive array of seeds here, particularly for greens, tomatoes, and peppers. They also sell seedlings, including tomatoes, peppers, eggplants, onions, leeks, herbs, berries, and sweet potatoes.

TOTALLY TOMATOES

RANDOLPH, WI; 800-345-5977; TOTALLYTOMATO.COM

The focus here, as the name implies, is on tomatoes—a long list of seeds and plants, with many heirlooms included. They also carry a wide array of sweet and hot peppers, garlic and onions, and various vegetable seeds.

VERMONT BEAN SEED CO.

RANDOLPH, WI; 800-349-1071; VERMONTBEAN.COM

That's right—beans! Lots of unusual vegetable seeds too, plus asparagus, herb, onion, tomato, pepper, horseradish, and Jerusalem artichoke plants.

WOOD PRAIRIE FARM

BRIDGEWATER, ME; 800-829-9765; WOODPRAIRIE.COM

They sell seeds for an organic, wild garden spring lettuce mix that is sublime! Their interesting mélange of offerings includes *lots* of seed potatoes, a huge list of vegetable seeds, garden tools, bagged potatoes, cooking supplies, and all kinds of grain mixtures for baking bread and muffins.

CHAPTER

4

FROM SOIL TO SEED

The best, most productive gardens evolve from the ground up, and rich, living soil is the foundation of their success. I'm going to show you why, what's down there, and how you can supercharge the natural action of the soil by mixing in some key elements before you plant. "Careful preparation is nine-tenths of success," my grandmother used to say, and this chapter provides the building blocks for the advance work: starting a compost pile, adding a worm bin, collecting the tools you'll need, and getting seeds ready to go in the ground.

Good soil is the foundation for healthy, productive plants.

'Fish' peppers, a pre-1870s African-American heirloom.

THE LOWDOWN ON DIRT

Three times a week, as I sell my heirloom seedlings at local farmers' markets, I have the same experience again and again, with only slight variations in the details. I'll notice someone eyeing my plants, strolling past my spot amid vendors of fresh-picked berries and tomatoes, surprised by the greenery sprawling from pots on the ground in front of me. I'll watch this person circle back, then stoop to read a few labels. It might be a dad with a toddler on his shoulders, a mom strollering a baby, a girl out for a shopping morning, her arms loaded with canvas bags.

I can already hear the questions coming.

"What *is* a 'Thai Green Pea' eggplant? I've never heard of that. And an 'Alabama Red' okra? *Okra* can be *red*?"

It's a snap to sell these people plants. In their minds, they're already in love with some oddball marvel, some *concept* of a vegetable, since there's no okra at all yet—my plants are babies. Still, the red okra, along with the green pea eggplant, hovers somewhere in a sun-lit realm of possibility, a place I happen to know well.

The mere mention of a rare or storied edible sends me there—which is partly how I've wound up peddling 'Chocolate Amazon' tomatoes and 'Canoe Creek Colossal' melons. At some point in the past, I stumbled on seeds for these and couldn't wait to get them in the ground, see how they grew, find out what the fruit looked like, see how it tasted.

At the same time, in this first moment with a smitten customer, as much as I yearn to share my treasures (I love my plants, every one), I might feel like holding back.

"What are you going to do with that?" I sometimes ask, before I can catch myself.

"Well, plant it," is the usual answer.

"In what?" I persist, like an anxious dog breeder screening potential buyers of his puppies.

The analogy isn't that far-fetched. Not only do I want my plants in good homes, I want people to be successful with them, to have the thrill of raising something delicious for the table instead of failing and then dismissing the whole idea.

Very often, I get answers that don't encourage me. Customers say they're going to put my beloved okra "in the ground," or, if pressed, "in dirt."

But do they know what kind of "dirt" they have? Can they tell the difference between "dirt" and "soil"?

Usually, their answers are "no," and "no," and suddenly, class swings into session. I can't sell plants without giving my little discourse on organic matter, that which separates soil from dirt. Because before you plant, you need to set up the conditions for your own success, and success begins with good soil.

Soil is the earth's wondrous, living blanket, a medium forged over eons of time by natural forces heaving and crashing against rocks, vegetation, animals. Vibrant and ever-changing, it teems with bacteria, fungi, mold, yeast, insects, worms, and other organisms—some not even visible—in almost unfathomable numbers.

SOIL BOOSTERS AND WHAT THEY DO

Alfalfa meal: adds small amounts of needed nitrogen, potassium, phosphorus, and trace minerals; conditions soil; stimulates beneficial soil organisms

Fishbone meal: great source of the phosphorus and calcium plants need

Greensand: As described in Peaceful Valley's catalog, this is sand mined from marine deposits millions of years old. Rich in trace elements and minerals, especially slow-release potassium, it's a good soil conditioner and stimulates beneficial soil microbes that make nutrients available to plants.

Low-nitrogen bat guano: very effective organic fertilizer; fast-acting, natural source of nutrients

Oyster shell lime: adjusts soil pH (we will discuss pH further in Chapter 5); conditions and loosens soil; adds micronutrients; promotes strong root growth

Soft rock phosphate: adds phosphorus, calcium, trace minerals

---

Dirt, on the other hand, is synonymous with something unclean. It might be little more than fine sand or leathery clay that holds scant nourishment for a root—if a root can even get through it. Sadly, dirt—hard-packed, windblown, or waterlogged—is what many of us have in our backyards. It's grim stuff, inhospitable to living things, unless we do something to change it.

THE FIX

To turn dirt into soil, you amend it with organic matter. This is what gardeners mean when they say, "Feed the soil, not the plant." If your soil is alive with busy beings eating and excreting, a wide range of nutrients will be available to your plants. The soil will be more permeable to roots and more water-retentive, and will do a better job of balancing acidity and alkalinity, an important factor for healthy growth.

So, when you plant vegetables in backyard ground, start by digging down a foot and mixing organic compost with your dirt at about a one-to-one ratio. At first, the compost you use will probably come in bags from a nursery and contain such things as decomposed leaves, mushroom bits, aged manure, and maybe seaweed. Whatever it is, it won't be nearly as good as what you can make yourself, eventually, but it's a place to start. Once it's in the ground, you're on your way to something great, and your soil is much improved.

But while some garden makers would stop there, I encourage you to push on with mineral, trace mineral, and microbial boosters until you've mixed up an ambrosia for your plants. You'll know it's worth it when you taste the harvest. True, you'll have to go a bit out of your way to do what I'm suggesting. A lot of super-soil foods aren't available at your local nursery. But you can find them all online, many from Peaceful Valley Farm & Garden Supply (groworganic.com). The ones I use, and the proportions I use them in, are those that I have found, through trial and error, work best for me. (See "Soil Boosters and What They Do," above.) In fact, I have developed a special soil-boosting recipe I call my HayGround fertilizer blend, and you will see mention of it often in the book. Other dedicated gardeners will have their own version of this recipe, and you may find, as you use it, that over time you begin to change it somewhat too. But it's quite good and complete in itself, and besides working well for amending soil, it's an excellent fertilizer.

For enriching soil, though, let's say you're working in a pretty typical, 4-by-6-foot backyard space. Once you've added the compost to your native dirt, you're going to mix up a batch of my HayGround fertilizer blend and then dig that into your bed too. Start with a wheelbarrow or large container, add the following ingredients, and blend well with a shovel: 4 cups of fishbone meal; 2 cups of greensand; and 6 cups each of oyster shell lime, soft rock phosphate, alfalfa meal, and aged, low-nitrogen bat guano, in a 3-10-1 formula (the numbers represent the formula's balance of nitrogen, phosphorus, and potassium). Working this into your ground will draw hungry creatures—including aerating, oxygenating earthworms—who will get to work making plant food.

If you opt instead to plant your vegetables in containers, or to grow them in raised beds, you will fill these initially with top-quality organic potting soil, such as my favorite, Edna's Best from E.B. Stone Organics. Whichever one you choose, read the label for additives like mycorrhizal fungi (beneficial organisms), worm castings, kelp meal, feather meal, washed sand, gypsum, and oyster shell lime. In most cases, with these in the mix, you won't need to amend further (or even add compost) until your plants have been in the ground for a month, or until it's time to switch out one crop for another.

At that point, when you have pulled and eaten your first spring radishes, for instance, and you decide to plant herbs in their place, stir up a batch of the HayGround blend and work about 3 tablespoons of it, along with some organic compost, into the soil around each new seedling to give it a good start. Do this each time a crop finishes and you start another.

Some gardeners, especially those in mild-winter climates, do two complete crop changeovers each year, removing all remnants of their cold-season vegetables in the spring and completely reprepping their beds, and repeating the process in fall after summer crops finish. Those who take this route should amend the soil after lifting spent plants with up to 50 percent organic compost and a full batch (in the amounts and proportions described above) of the HayGround blend. If possible, to get the microbial action going before replanting, let the bed rest then for a week to 10 days, watering daily.

Susan and Rob's compost tumblers.

If this is sounding too complicated, remember: You can start modestly, with just a plant or two—and organic potting soil—in a container. In my experience, one small success is irresistible. A nice haul of tomatoes brings customers back, wanting to broaden their operation, try more plants, and get their children into the act. Before long, as they start to understand (and *appreciate*) soil, the conversation inevitably turns to compost.

CAVIAR FOR CAULIFLOWER

When I was little, the compost pile obsessed me. Even in winter, when the ground was snowy, I could pull off the cover and feel the heat rising from its center. I could poke in a stick and

Six soil boosters mix it up in my HayGround organic blend, which I think of as ambrosia for plants.

SOIL IS THE EARTH'S WONDROUS,
LIVING BLANKET, A MEDIUM FORGED OVER
EONS OF TIME BY NATURAL FORCES
HEAVING AND CRASHING AGAINST ROCKS,
VEGETATION, ANIMALS.

The worm composter in my garden is a hotbed of activity!

stir up worms. Where did that heat come from? How did it transform the pile, making all the old corn husks and tomato vines we had heaped on it disappear? How did the worms stay alive down there? What created the rich, black, sweet crumbs that we unearthed each spring and carted to the garden to scatter on the beds and make the food grow?

Like many children I've met since, I gave these questions a lot of thought. Turning them over in my mind, I saw myself as having entered into a mysterious partnership with nature. I did a few things, nature did the rest—presto! I felt strangely important but also humbled by the power of the earth, which had revealed itself, privately, to me.

I've never lost my fascination with the simple beauty of the process. In fact, a compost pile is one of the first subjects

I discuss with my design clients. Where and how can we get one going? Since this depends on the size and configuration of the property—and in city gardens, there often isn't much room to spare—the answer tends to be simple.

Some people choose compact, user-friendly compost tumblers, which can be tucked out of sight in a sunny nook behind a garage. These have a clear advantage over the sort of passive pile I grew up with: If you don't have all winter to wait while your compost cooks, and you can't be troubled to turn it with a pitchfork, you can spin your tumbler around to mix up the ingredients and introduce the oxygen that bacteria need to break down those ingredients.

What I prefer is even simpler and, like the tumbler, is available through Internet sources. It's a molded-plastic,

I see my worms as small but mighty members of my garden team.

IF YOU REALLY WANT TO HOOK YOUR CHILD AND START HIM OR HER EARLY ON THE GARDENING PATH, TRY WORMS.

A worm bin with a spigot for "tea."

3-foot-square bin with four sides, a locking top, and an open bottom. You throw in an 8-inch layer of grass clippings, another 8 inches of dry leaves, and your saved-up vegetable scraps. Sprinkle on a couple of handfuls of alfalfa meal, finish with a 2-inch layer of potting soil and a dose of compost activator (Peaceful Valley makes a good one called Bio-Dynamic Compost Inoculant), and repeat the process. In as little as a month, especially if you mix or "turn" it, you'll have the best manna in the world for plants.

THE HEROIC WORM

Like me, kids tend to be taken with compost and gain from it, painlessly, important insights into the living world.

But if you really want to hook your child and start him or her early on the gardening path, try worms.

In the last few years, worm bins have gained on compost as the method du jour for feeding soil. Forget the prejudices you might have toward creepy-crawlies. Worm bins are cleaner, more contained, and, in some cases, smaller than many compost set-ups, and they sit in shade rather than sun. Not unlike a multilayered vegetable steamer, they provide perforated tiers of food for the worms, which mow through them, leaving "castings" behind as they move on to fresh levels.

If you become a worm farmer, your job will be to fill the tiers weekly with vegetable scraps and greens and collect the castings as soil additives for your garden-to-be. Not only will your beds be richer in nutrients, but your plants will be more resistant to certain chewing insects.

And if that's not enough, many worm bins are equipped with a spigot that lets you tap the liquid that sinks to the bottom tier. This "worm tea" is an organic gardener's black gold. Dilute it to one-fifth strength with water and spray it on the leaves of edibles to boost yield and reduce pests.

All in all, earthworms and their by-products are among our finest allies in building soil. They increase microbial content and water conductivity, they help balance soil pH, and they reduce parasitic nematodes that weaken and kill plants.

One note of caution: While I'll give you other reasons elsewhere in this book to shun non-organic chemical fertilizers, here's a big one—they'll send your worms packing.

A TRIP TO THE TOOL SHED

Just as it's wise to consider soil before you plant, it's smart to arm yourself with tools. You might not need many, but the right ones can cut your work time in half and make it so much more pleasant. A good hoe, for instance, speeds weeding. A long-handled cultivator reduces back strain while loosening soil around plants' roots.

In my grandmother's shed, every implement had its place. A simple, pine-frame structure with a packed-earth floor, her shed was lined with shelves for her seed jars and hand tools, and there was a system of pegs for hanging hoes and shovels. Her wheelbarrow sat in a corner, and a small table provided her—and me—with a sheltered spot for planting out the seedlings that would give us a jump on spring growing.

In my own day-to-day operation, I use the same basic tools she used. These, to me, are the essentials that every food gardener needs:

Flat shovel: for moving materials, such as sand or compost, from a container or wheelbarrow to a bed

Garden hook: for weeding, making seed rows, working in compost

Garden hose: for putting water where you need it

Hand pruners: for trimming/pruning smaller plants

Long-handled, four-pronged cultivator: for loosening soil and working air around plants

Long-handled spade: for transplanting; for digging holes

Loppers: for cutting large branches

Metal rake: for making rows, and leveling and cleaning soil

Pickax: for breaking up hard soil and mixing in amendments

Pitch fork: for digging and turning soil or compost

Pump sprayers, at least two: for foliar feeding and control of pests and fungus

Soil scoop: for planting

Watering can: for smaller irrigation jobs

Wheelbarrow: for transporting anything large, heavy, or unwieldy around the garden; for mixing up soil amendments

SUPER SEEDS

In the last chapter, I talked about the choice of planting seeds or seedlings, and I admitted that despite the fact that I *sell* seedlings, I think every gardener should try both, and even grow both. Why? Because though seedlings get you to the harvest faster, seeds are fun, they're miraculous, and they give you a ringside seat at the dawn of being.

I won't tell you to sow your seeds, or at least most of them, directly in the ground. If you do, you might lose more than you grow to feeding birds and other critters. I *will* tell you to do what Eloise and I did—sow them in seed trays, 4-inch pots, or 6-packs; grow them until they're 2 or 3 inches tall and rooted; choose the best of the bunch; and plant *these* in the ground.

To begin with, you're going to give your seeds a big advantage by soaking them in something called a bio-stimulant. This will lead to a healthier plant that sprouts faster, resists disease better, and yields a larger crop.

My preferred formula includes 4 tablespoons Agri-Gro (a concentrated micronutrient food by a company of the same name that you can find on the Web), ½ teaspoon Dark Energy (an amino acid blend by GreenSpirit Hydrogardens), 1 teaspoon ThermX 70 (a wetting agent and plant food from Biocontrol Network), and 1 cup of worm or compost tea, all mixed into 1 gallon of water. (You can order all these products online.)

Small, soft seeds, like those of eggplant and tomatoes, need only a 2-hour soaking. Those with harder coats (okra, beets, chard, hot peppers) must be soaked overnight. (Of course, to avoid mixing up your seeds, you will soak each type separately.) While they soak, you can prepare your containers and soil.

To protect your new plants from rot and fungus, first rinse any containers you're reusing in a solution of 1 tablespoon of bleach stirred into 1 gallon of water. Next, fill them with a half-and-half blend of good-quality potting soil and vermiculite or perlite (both super-heated mineral products that decrease soil density and promote good drainage). Then, to further discourage fungal problems, mix up a home-style soil treatment I learned from Eloise: Steep 2 cups of loose chamomile tea in boiling water for 20 minutes and add 1 tablespoon of apple cider vinegar. Strain the tea, pour it into a watering can, and use it to soak the soil in your containers.

Finally, pluck the seeds out of their nutrient baths and plant each at the depth that's recommended for its type. Put your pots where the sun is bright but gentle, and check them often so you'll know exactly when the miracle has happened.

A SIMPLE, PINE-FRAME STRUCTURE WITH A PACKED-EARTH FLOOR, MY GRANDMOTHER'S TOOL SHED WAS LINED WITH SHELVES FOR HER SEED JARS AND HAND TOOLS, AND THERE WAS A SYSTEM OF PEGS FOR HANGING HOES AND SHOVELS.

The tools from *my* toolshed.

CHAPTER

5

MAKING YOUR BEDS AND CHOOSING BEDMATES

In this chapter, I'll talk about my two favorite types of beds, how to choose which is right for you, and how to make it. I'll also discuss garden watering, which you'll need to think about at the construction stage, and then planting: What's going in, where, how, and with what companions. This is a moment I especially love—as the garden begins to take shape!

A simple seating cap makes it easy to tend raised beds without stooping.

BUILDING BEDS:
GOING UP VS. GOING DOWN

There are many ways to start a garden. Right now, having decided on a location, roughed out dimensions, gotten some seedlings going, and stockpiled potting soil, you're on the verge of plunging in. Maybe you've already opted to start with pots, filling them with the herbs and lettuce we discussed in Chapter 2. Or you've decided to plant directly in your back-yard's ground, after first digging it a foot deep and adding good organic compost at a 1-to-1 ratio with your dirt—an approach described in Chapter 4 (see page 66). If you're more ambitious and want to take your garden to another level, you'll find two of the easiest methods among the best for growing food.

The first involves constructing what is, really, a giant, above-ground container for top-quality organic potting soil. The second creates a similar container for the same soil *below* the ground, though with a frame of earth (an excavated pit) instead of wood or stone.

In both cases, you grow your vegetables in great soil—at least 18 inches of it—rather than plunking them straight into a mix of native garden earth and compost. Either way, you begin by breaking up the ground, so even where the plants' roots meet that native earth, they'll have a smoother time of pushing through it. Early spadework opens and loosens heavy, compacted soil (the kind most of us have) and encourages deep, healthy roots that can reach for nutrients they need.

In my experience, both above- and below-ground "raised" beds are equally good ways to produce strong, productive plants. Choosing between them is mostly a question of aes-thetics, comfort, and cost. For some people, framed beds have a neater look. If you finish them with a seating cap, they're a snap to tend without bending, so they're easier on your back. However, they're also more expensive and involved, since you have to buy construction materials and either assemble them yourself or pay someone to do it for you.

EARLY SPADEWORK OPENS AND LOOSENS HEAVY, COMPACTED SOIL (THE KIND MOST OF US HAVE) AND ENCOURAGES DEEP, HEALTHY ROOTS.

STURDY, SEMI-PERMANENT, AND EASY TO USE, A RAISED BED WILL START YOU OFF RIGHT.

So before you go in one direction or the other, evaluate your garden goals concerning appearance, convenience, and budget. As you continue to garden, your goals may change, and you can always alter your methods then. Besides trying another kind of bed, you might want to experiment with different materials, edging your plot with galvanized metal, pole fencing, or large-scale pottery shards. You could decide to change your garden's location, and in the new spot, follow a friend's advice instead of mine for preparing the ground. It's exciting to swap ideas with other gardeners, and to pore through great garden books (for example, John Jeavons' masterwork, *How to Grow More Vegetables,* or my all-time top pick, William Woys Weaver's *Heirloom Vegetable Gardening*).

For right now, though, the methods I'm describing, besides being effective, are among the simplest, and simple is good when you're beginning.

Option 1: Going High

Sturdy, semi-permanent, and easy to use, a raised bed will start you off right. In terms of expense, remember that the cost of rot-resistant wooden beds, which can last for several decades, is up-front money you will spend once and very possibly not again. Of course, you can certainly spend *more,* if you have a carpenter make your beds, or if you use other materials. Hiring a mason to construct the same bed out of stacked or poured concrete can quintuple the cost, and stacked stone might run twice as much as concrete. Your materials will depend somewhat on the style of your house—and whether you care if your garden fits with it—and just *how long* you want your beds to be around. In both cost and durability, stone and concrete represent sizable commitments to edible gardening.

Constructing raised beds out of wood, which many people choose to do, is a relatively simple job. But if you're all thumbs with building tools, you can make it even simpler. A good online source, Naturalyards.com, sells rot-resistant cedar bed kits, which arrive in the form of slats that snap together in a matter of minutes. If you're more confident in the DIY department, you can do what I do: Go to a local lumberyard, choose some farmed redwood or cedar boards (both hold up better than other woods in damp conditions), and have them cut to size.

For me, building is part of the fun of gardening. I *like* loading my pockets with deck screws and sorting tools to pick the right ones for the job. The smell of fresh-cut wood fills my head with ideas, and I couldn't be happier, especially if I'm sharing the work with my son or daughter. *That,* I know, is a key memory from their childhood—helping me reel out measuring tape, mark boards with a pencil, and screw in bolts while we chattered over every step. When you build something with your children (or girlfriend, or brother, for that matter), you have a chance to get to know each other better as you face challenges as a team. Some of my best discussions with my kids have happened in the garden, over heaped boards and bagged soil.

If you do go the DIY route, don't forget that board dimensions aren't exact. A 12-inch width is usually more like 11½ inches, so figure the difference into your calculations. On a first project, keep things basic. Have the lumberyard cut your boards and even miter the corners of the cap, unless you're experienced with a saw. In fact, my building instructions are intended not as a carpentry lesson, but rather as a template for a simple concept you can alter to fit your situation.

Some of the raised beds in my growing grounds have wire supports for the tomatoes.

PUTTING IT TOGETHER

Picture a 4-by-6-foot bottomless wooden crate of either cedar or farmed redwood. Each of its sides is two boards high; each board is bolted at the end to a thick, square corner post; each long side is further stabilized at its midpoint with an additional 2-by-4-inch post. That's what I'm proposing here, and to begin with, you'll go to the lumberyard for supplies.

FRAME MATERIALS
FOUR 2" X 12" X 6' BOARDS
FOUR 2" X 12" X 4' BOARDS
FOUR 4" X 4" X 24" CORNER POSTS
TWO 2" X 4" X 24" STABILIZING SIDE POSTS, CUT TO A POINT
FORTY-EIGHT 4½" GALVANIZED DECK SCREWS (FOR CORNERS)
TEN 3½" GALVANIZED DECK SCREWS (FOR LONG SIDES)

CAP MATERIALS
TWO 2" X 6" X 4' BOARDS
TWO 2" X 6" X 6' BOARDS
SIXTEEN 4½" GALVANIZED DECK SCREWS (FOR CORNERS)
FOUR 3½" GALVANIZED DECK SCREWS (FOR LONG SIDES)

STEP 1. PREPPING THE GROUND

Even a raised bed, which you will initially load with excellent potting soil, requires some ground-level preparation. Because the roots of many edibles run deep, you want to make sure they meet good, loose soil even below the bed. Still, since they will travel through at least 18 inches of the potting soil to get there, you only need to dig down an additional foot (which gives roots 2½ feet of total depth) to break up your ground, using a shovel or pickax. When the soil is loose, add 5 pounds of granular gypsum, a mineral compound that further opens up the soil, and 5 bags (about 1½ cubic feet, and about 20 pounds each, depending on the brand) of organic compost. Shovel and mix these together evenly, then soak the whole mixture thoroughly with a hose.

STEP 2. BUILDING YOUR FRAME

Pick an outdoor spot, separate from where you've prepped your bed, where you have room to spread out. Measure and mark each board end to indicate where 3 evenly spaced screws will attach the board to a corner post, and pre-drill the holes. Line up the boards with the posts, one by one, and attach them with the screws until your frame is complete.

STEP 3. PLACING THE BED

Fit the garden bed frame over the prepared plot, then work a shovel gently around it from both sides, so that the frame settles firmly into the soil, leaving about 18 inches above the ground. Add the stabilizing posts at the midway point on each long side (on the inside of the frame), use a mallet to pound them in (to about 3 inches below the top of the frame), and attach the side boards to them, using 5 screws per post.

STEP 4. CAPPING IT OFF

After using a level to make sure all sides are the same height, top the bed off with your flat, 2-inch-thick seating cap, and screw its mitered corners from the top into the corner posts. Secure each side with an additional screw.

STEP 5. FINISHING UP

Fill the frame to the top with potting soil and plant. If you plan to use drip irrigation, leave 4 to 6 inches of space between the soil and the top of the bed, so you can lay in drip tubes before the bed is full (see "Drip Demystified," page 87).

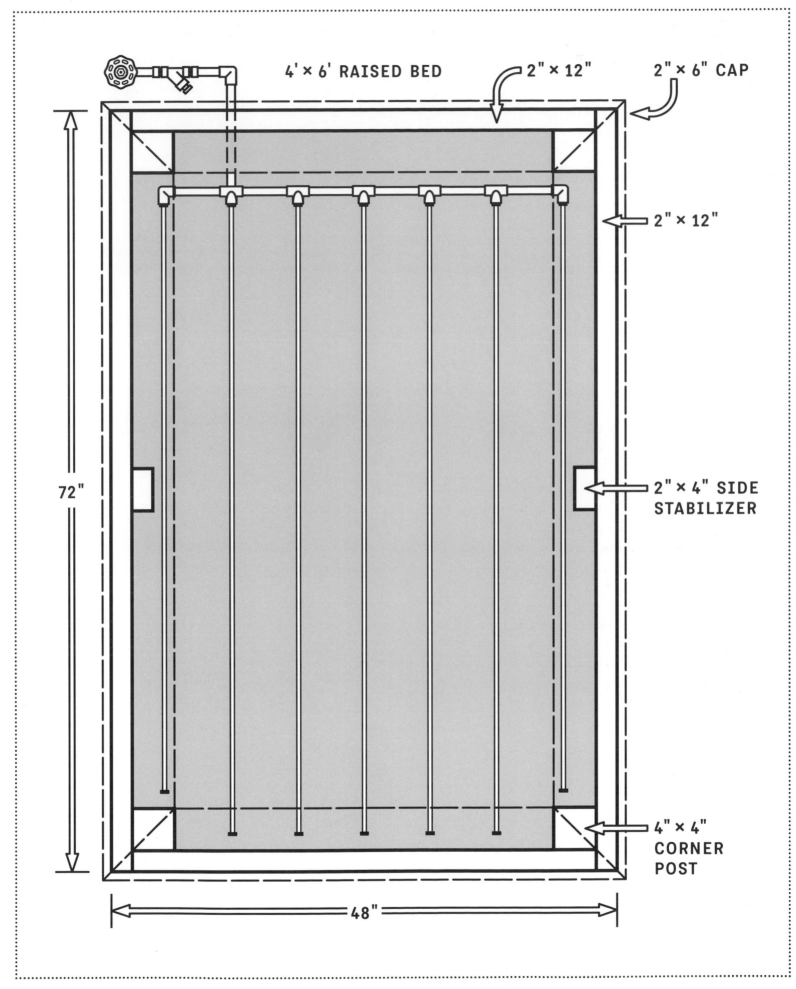

4' × 6' RAISED BED

2" × 12"

2" × 6" CAP

2" × 12"

2" × 4" SIDE STABILIZER

72"

4" × 4" CORNER POST

48"

Raised beds can take the form of basic, 18-inch-high rectangles (above), or you can alter their shapes to fit irregular spaces, as I did in John and Diane Hertz's garden (below).

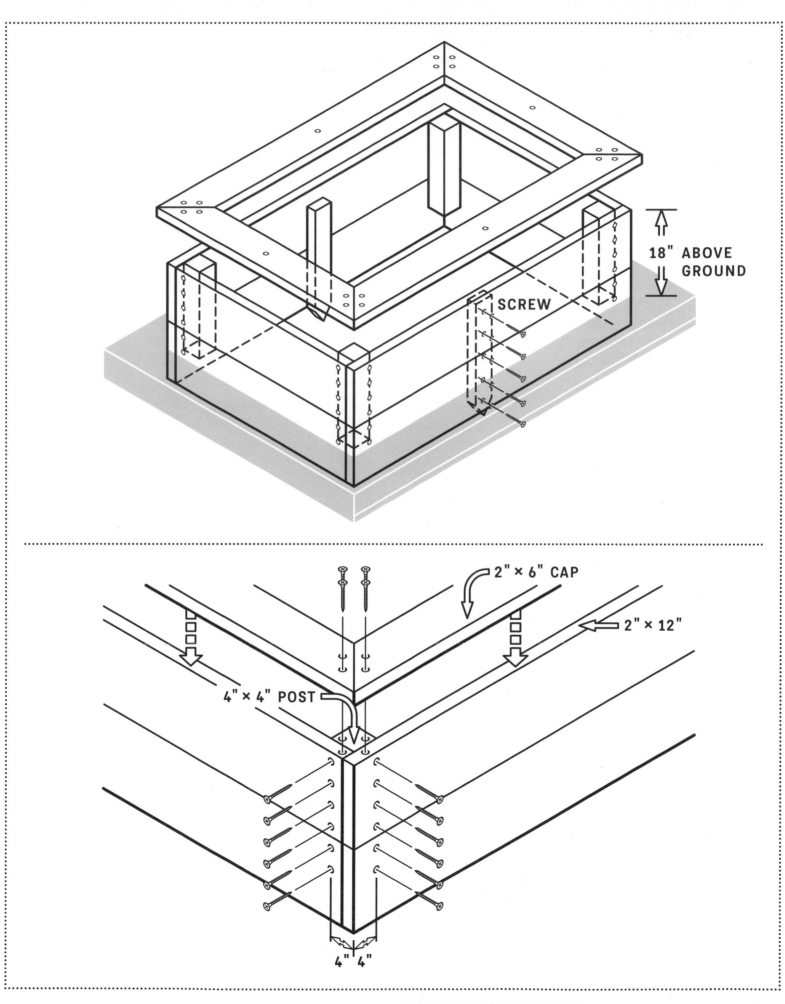

18" ABOVE
GROUND

SCREW

2" × 6" CAP

2" × 12"

4" × 4" POST

4"   4"

Option 2: Digging Deep

For an even easier and less pricey bed, you can do what my grandmother did, and we Williams children grew up doing with her: Forego the frame altogether and make what I call "underground raised beds" (see "The Underground Scoop," opposite). These too are containers, though they go below rather than above the surface of the soil.

You can create underground raised beds in just about any sunny spot that's located near a water source. We used to begin ours with already established beds, but they're almost as easy to start from scratch. What we did each fall, under Eloise's supervision, was to dig all the soil out of each of her beds, to a depth of about 1 foot. Heaping the soil at one end, we'd fill our pits with the leaves, compost, and grass clippings that were plentiful around her place, and then we'd shovel the soil back on top and cover it with boards or plastic. Come spring, when we pulled the covering off, steam rose from the beds, and they were full of earthworms and ready to plant. I remember growing 12-foot okra plants in beds prepared this way!

If you're a new gardener—or one who hasn't grown food in awhile—it might be a good idea to start with this sort of bed. Once you discover, as I predict you will, how satisfying vegetable gardening is, and you know you're going to stick with it, you can build true raised beds later.

alfalfa meal, washed sand, and mycorrhizal fungi make for stronger, more disease- and pest-resistant plants that produce more and better food.

True, there *are* commercial potting mixes that contain little more than ground-up bark, peat moss, and perlite, but I don't recommend you fill your beds with these. As I advised in the last chapter, read labels for ingredients to ensure adequate plant nutrition from soil that holds moisture but drains well too. Don't forget, you're investing in your own success—not to mention, saving yourself the early effort of tracking down and mixing in specific additives yourself. That part comes later, when your beds need feeding and refreshing.

If the price of bagged soil still seems too high, you can skip raised *or* underground raised beds at first and just dig your ground well and deeply, enriching it generously with 50 percent good organic compost and my HayGround fertilizer blend (page 66). Alternatively, it may be possible to find quality, local organic potting soil by the truckload. Consult your nearest Cooperative Extension office for potential sources, and get to know your neighborhood nursery, where certified experts might have other recommendations. You'll have to wheelbarrow delivered soil from your street or driveway to your garden bed, but you'll get more of it for much less than the bagged product costs.

REMINDER: DON'T SKIMP ON SOIL

I can't say it enough: Great soil is fundamental to a great garden. It's your most important investment, and it's a big one. Potting soil for a raised bed is pricey, especially the one I like most (Edna's Best, from E.B. Stone Organics), and it takes about 30 bags to fill a 4-by-6-foot, 18-inch-high bed.

Why should you pay a lot to *buy* something that looks so similar to what's lying around outside, in such huge quantities, for *free*? Because, as discussed in Chapter 4, there's a big difference between backyard dirt and top-quality organic potting soils. These premium mixes not only lack the weed seeds, pests, and pathogens that might lurk in your own dirt, but they contain abundant plant nutrients, soil conditioners, beneficial organisms, and other building blocks of a *living* medium for growth. Their pH levels fall within the optimal range for edibles (see "pH: What's That?," opposite page). Taken together, their respective (and varying) formulas of organic composts, earthworm castings, aged manures, gypsum,

WATERING: TO HOSE OR NOT TO HOSE

As I said earlier, drip irrigation goes in during a late stage of bed construction. That means that I need to talk about water now instead of putting it off until I get to plant care.

So here is where I state my case *against* drip. I believe that the best way to water veggies is the old-fashioned way: by hand. I say this even knowing what I know—that most people are too busy to water, which is one of the most common causes of garden failure.

When you carry a hose or watering can from plant to plant, you're much likelier to give each one what it needs. Celery, for instance, craves a lot more moisture than a native Mediterranean herb like rosemary or thyme. Tomatoes require less water as they fruit and ripen; give them too much then and they'll start to crack and grow watery and tasteless. True, it's death to a garden if you don't water at all (especially in summer-dry spots like Southern California), but it's nearly as

pH: WHAT'S THAT?

In simple terms, pH is the measure of acidity or alkalinity in your soil, and it's important because it affects how plants take up soil nutrients. The value of soil pH is expressed in numerical terms, from 0 to 14, with 7 being neutral, 0 to 7 falling in the acidic range, and numbers above 7 indicating alkalinity. Most edibles do best in slightly acid to neutral territory; the preferred pH range for lettuce, squash, and asparagus is 6.0 to 7.0; corn, 5.5 to 6.8; and celery, 6.5 to 7.5.

When you do raised-bed gardening, you start with good organic potting soils that contain pH adjustors. Edna's Best, for one, includes oyster shell lime and dolomite lime, which keep its pH around 6.5, right in the zone vegetables like.

But even if you're planting directly in your native soil, you can adjust the pH yourself. The first step is to either buy a soil-test kit at a garden center or contact your local Cooperative Extension office for a list of soil-testing labs you can take a sample to. When you know your soil's pH, you can add lime to make it more alkaline, or ground rock sulphur to make it more acidic. Generously amending soil with organic compost also helps keep pH in balance.

THE UNDERGROUND SCOOP

STEP 1. DIGGING DOWN
Begin, say, with a 4-by-6-foot piece of ground you've already cleared of weeds. When you dig it for the first time (or the first time in ages), work it with a pickax to break up its hard layers.

STEP 2. TOSSING TIRED DIRT
Shovel to a depth of 1½ to 2 feet, throw the soil into a wheelbarrow, and get rid of it. (I do this by dumping it elsewhere in my yard—in a low spot, say, where I need some extra elevation.)

STEP 3. KEEP WORKING IT
Turn the soil in the bed's bottom a bit more with your spade, then add 5 pounds of granular gypsum to further loosen the soil, and 5 bags of organic compost (about 1½ cubic feet, and about 20 pounds each, depending on the brand). Shovel and mix these together evenly and soak them with a hose.

STEP 4. FILL 'ER UP
Load the pit with potting soil, as you would a pot, mounding it a little higher than the surrounding ground, and you're ready to plant.

WHEN YOU BUILD SOMETHING WITH YOUR CHILDREN (OR GIRLFRIEND, OR BROTHER, FOR THAT MATTER), YOU HAVE A CHANCE TO GET TO KNOW EACH OTHER BETTER AS YOU FACE CHALLENGES AS A TEAM.

bad to put all your edibles on automatic sprinklers, set the timer, and walk away. In nature, one size never fits all, and you learn this fast when you're growing food.

Another reason to hand water is that it forces you to pay attention. As you move in to aim a gentle spray at plants' roots (rather than at leaves, where lingering water can lead to fungus), you'll observe which ones are getting chewed, and by what, so you can do something about it. Which are fruiting? What needs picking? Which plants are just plain *beautiful* today? If you're not looking, you won't see.

The early morning is the time I like to commune with plants—a time, not surprisingly, when I'm not ready to talk to *people*. At 6 A.M., a ruffly, aromatic basil can remind me of how good it is to be alive. Lucky for me, early morning is the best time to grab the hose; water early and whatever moisture *does*

hit plants' leaves has a chance to dry out in the sun. In the cool morning, water soaks nicely into the soil, while later on, in midday heat, it evaporates so fast that you waste a lot of it.

Closely watching what you grow helps you take care of it. A wilting plant is often telling you it needs water. If you're unsure—since overwatering can be dangerous too—poke your finger down an inch around the plant's root zone. If it feels damp, don't water; if it's dry, it's time.

Hand watering is a simple, peaceful task. It involves little equipment, initial planning, or expense. In contrast, you have to think ahead—and budget for—automatic irrigation, which you must install yourself, or pay someone to install, adding hundreds of dollars, potentially, to your budget. Hand water, and you'll pay a fraction of that cost for a good hose and a few attachments.

In the Hertz garden in Malibu, we planted the first vegetables on a steep hillside already sectioned into narrow beds with landscape ties.

DRIP DEMYSTIFIED

For some gardeners, a drip watering system literally makes a garden possible. Since it's buried underground, you lay it in before you fill your beds entirely with soil. The system I like, which has built-in anti-clog features and a comprehensive illustrated Web site, is Netafim (www.netafimusa.com). It's not hard to install if you can dig a trench and fit some simple parts together, but you can certainly hire a landscape contractor or irrigation specialist to do the work.

Basically, to get started, you need to bring a water line to your planting bed, which requires digging a trench from the water source (such as a hose bib by the house) and laying down a PVC (polyvinyl chloride) pipe, in a minimum thickness that's referred to as Schedule 40. You bury the pipe 8 to 12 inches underground, after first fitting it, near the hose bib, with a combination pressure-regulator and filter (to control waterflow and keep the system from clogging). At the far end of the trench, where it meets the bed, you'll connect your pipe using a linking piece called an elbow joint, to a second, perpendicular pipe at one edge of the bed. This second pipe rises to a point about 6 inches below the bed's top. There, you'll attach it to a third PVC pipe that

extends from one end to the other along one short side of your bed. Every 12 inches along this third pipe, you cut in a T-connector to attach a drip tube that runs the length of the bed. Lastly, cap the end of each tube and anchor each in place with a series of staples.

When all tubes are in place, cover them with the rest of the bed's soil (your drip tubing should be 4 to 6 inches below the finished soil level), and you're in business. For convenience, and to take full advantage of your system, you'll probably add a timer, so you can set the water to come on automatically. But even with a timer, you should keep an eye on plants and be ready to spot-water whatever needs it, or reduce the water when plants are getting too much. Remember the finger test: One inch down, your soil shouldn't be either bone-dry or soggy.

Note: Gardeners in regions with icy winters will need to shut off the water to the drip system before the first freeze, drain the system, and wrap any exposed pipe with insulation tape, a yearly ritual that's well explained on the web, at dripirrigation.com/drip_irrigation_help.php?pgv=Article13.

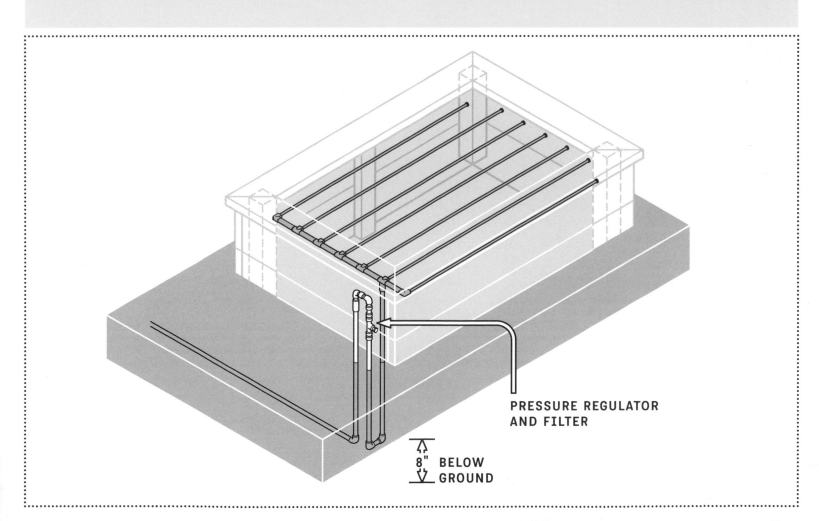

PRESSURE REGULATOR
AND FILTER

8" BELOW GROUND

My favorite brand is a black Craftsman hose from Sears. It tolerates very high (180-degree) heat, you can lay it down on baking concrete, and it has a lifetime guarantee. I like to use mine with one of two attachments, either a watering wand, which has soft spray action and can get in close to the base of a plant, or a fan-shaped sprayer. The sprayer is best for larger areas and bigger jobs—for example, if you spot an aphid infestation. This is one instance when you *will* want to hose down leaves, and blast them hard, to send bugs packing.

Ideally, if I have a few extra minutes, I always scratch lightly around each plant with my single-prong garden hook before I water. This boosts absorption. I wait for moisture to soak in, then I water again, since hitting plants twice each time lets me water less often.

BURIED TREASURE: DRIP IRRIGATION

As I've said, many people—and most of my clients—have trouble finding time to water. Many, at least early on, feel more comfortable with a watering system. In a food garden, the best choice is underground drip. In my experience, spray irrigation and vegetables don't mix. Spray heads direct too much water at leaves. They're inexact and wasteful, and thus a much less environmentally friendly option. Drip tubes, buried 4 to 6 inches deep and equipped with tiny emitters, put moisture just where plants need it, around their roots. Of course, they also create an invisible network that you risk digging up if you're not careful and forget it's there. Some pitchfork-happy friends of mine have given up on drip as a result, but the trade-off works for them. Like me, they've made watering a ritual that they actually look forward to.

BOON COMPANIONS: PAIRING PLANTS

Now we're getting to the fun part, where, having built the set and hung the curtains, we bring the actors onstage. We've got our seedlings. Some of us have sketches. We've considered aspects of plant relationships: Some get big and will steal the light from others, while some don't mind being overshadowed. Lettuce, for instance, welcomes protection from taller beets.

But plant-world intrigues run deeper. Some plain don't *want* to be around others, while the opposite is also true: Among plants, some marriages are made in heaven.

There are practical explanations. Plants may compete for the same nutrients or attract the same pests, which spells trouble for both. Closely related edibles (such as tomatoes and peppers) may grow well together but have similar susceptibilities to disease and so are better off separated. Some plants secrete substances that ward *off* other plants' pests. Or their proximity makes another plant taste better, as chives seem to do for carrots and chervil for radishes. Some, like fennel, have a lot of antagonists; others (such as lettuce and eggplant) have none. Beans contribute loads of nitrogen to the soil, while corn eats nitrogen like candy, so these are complementary bedmates. Borage, a tall, aromatic herb, repels tomato worms and fits happily in a tomato patch. Basil's welcome too: It wards off flies that lay eggs on tomato leaves and also, reportedly, improves tomato flavor. Peas grow badly around onions. Planted together, pole beans and beets grow smaller than they do alone. Marigolds repel such a slew of bugs, they're beneficial in just about any company. Flowers, in general, and herbs like bee balm, thyme, and mint draw bees that stick around to pollinate the other edibles.

A lot has been written on these botanical relationships, and I've included a list, "Some Edible Friends and Foes" (opposite), so you can pick out some of the main, and most useful, ones at a glance. Trust your own observations of how plants grow too, and what makes them grow better. I'm sure you'll discover that, in the garden, as in the rest of life, breaking up big cliques of one population and integrating them with others promotes health and well-being. A whole tomato bed draws tomato predators in droves. Diversify that bed, throw in carrots, celery, and parsley, along with basil and borage, and those pests will find it harder to attack.

SOME EDIBLE FRIENDS AND FOES

Some plants, like lettuce, celery, and peppers, have special friends but no real garden antagonists, which makes them easy to fit in just about anywhere. Others, like members of the onion and cabbage families, are a bit more choosy, and so require extra consideration as you figure out where to put them.

ARTICHOKES
FRIENDS: sunflowers, tarragon

ASPARAGUS
FRIENDS: basil, parsley, tomatoes

BEAN FAMILY
FRIENDS: beets (only to bush beans), cabbage (only to bush beans), carrots, celery, chard, corn, cucumbers, eggplant, lettuce, marigolds, nasturtiums, radishes, rosemary, strawberries (only to bush beans), summer savory
FOES: beets (only to pole beans), garlic, onions

BEET FAMILY
FRIENDS: bush beans, cabbage, garlic, kohlrabi, lettuce, onions
FOE: pole beans

CABBAGE FAMILY (BROCCOLI, BRUSSELS SPROUTS, CABBAGE, CAULIFLOWER, COLLARDS, KALE, KOHLRABI)
FRIENDS: beets, celery, chard, cucumbers, garlic, lettuce, mint, nasturtiums, onions, potatoes, rosemary, sage, spinach, thyme
FOES: pole beans, strawberries, tomatoes

CARROTS
FRIENDS: beans, chives, garlic, lettuce, marigolds, onions, peas, peppers, radishes, rosemary, sage, tomatoes
FOE: dill

CELERY
FRIENDS: beans, cabbage, cauliflower, nasturtiums, onions, spinach, tomatoes

CORN
FRIENDS: beans, cucumbers, melons, parsley, peas, potatoes, pumpkins, squash
FOE: tomatoes

CUCUMBERS
FRIENDS: beans, cabbage, corn, lettuce, marigolds, nasturtiums, onions, peas, radishes, tomatoes
FOES: potatoes, sage (and aromatic herbs in general)

EGGPLANT
FRIENDS: beans, marigolds, mint, peppers, spinach, thyme

LETTUCE
FRIENDS: beans, beets, cabbage, carrots, chives, cucumbers, dill, garlic, onions, radishes, strawberries

MELONS
FRIENDS: corn, marigolds, nasturtiums, oregano, pumpkins, radishes, squash

ONION FAMILY
FRIENDS: beets, cabbage, carrots, celery, chard, cucumbers, dill, lettuce, peppers, squash, strawberries, summer savory, tomatoes
FOES: beans, peas, sage

PEAS
FRIENDS: carrots, chives, corn, cucumbers, mint, radishes, turnips
FOES: garlic, onions

PEPPERS
FRIENDS: basil, carrots, eggplant, onions

POTATOES
FRIENDS: beans, corn, cabbage
FOES: squash, cucumbers, tomatoes

RADISHES
FRIENDS: beans, carrots, chervil, cucumbers, garlic, lettuce, melons, nasturtiums, peas, spinach, squash
FOE: hyssop

SQUASHES
FRIENDS: borage, corn, marigolds, melons, nasturtiums, onions, radishes
FOE: Irish potatoes

STRAWBERRIES AND OTHER BUSH BERRIES
FRIENDS: borage, bush beans, lettuce, onions, spinach, thyme
FOE: cabbage

TOMATOES
FRIENDS: asparagus, basil, borage, carrots, celery, cucumbers, onions, parsley
FOES: cabbage, corn, kohlrabi, mature dill, potatoes

The face of summer: Blooming sunflowers in a vegetable patch

PICTURE DRIFTS OF PURPLE-LEAFED
EGGPLANT AND ORANGE PEPPERS, OR
SCALLOPED LETTUCE HEADS MINGLING
WITH FERNY CARROT TOPS.

What's more, mixed plantings are often wonderful to look at. Picture drifts of purple-leafed eggplant and orange peppers, or scalloped lettuce heads mingling with ferny carrot tops.

Some people just naturally group together the foods they like to eat. It's interesting how many turn out to be compatible.

PLANTING: TUCKING THEM IN

One of the most valuable lessons I learned from my grandmother was to start vegetable seeds in pots and then transplant them as seedlings into my beds, a practice that cuts way down on crop failure and one that many of you have already chosen to follow too. There are exceptions to this general rule, as I mentioned in Chapter 3, and they include carrots, radishes, and lettuce, all eager growers that sprout fast and make you feel like an experienced farmer as you watch their tiny rows appear.

What we haven't discussed yet are two important considerations concerning the planting process itself: How far apart do you space your seeds and seedlings, and how deep do you plant them? Seed packets always list this information, which varies from plant to plant and is crucial to their development. I will go into it further for each plant in Chapter 8 ("The Edible A-List of Must-Have Vegetables, Herbs, and Fruit"), but for now, here are a few examples that illustrate how plant-specific these guidelines are.

First, when you start seeds in a pot, you plant the seeds closer together and more shallowly than you will place the resulting seedlings in your bed. It just makes sense: As roots and leaves develop, plants need more room. If you started beet seeds, for example, you might have planted up to 4 seeds per inch of pot space at a depth of only ¼ inch. When you set out beet seedlings in your bed, though, you will space plants 4 inches apart, and bury about ½ inch of stem.

To give you a sense of how the spacing needs of plants compare, eggplant seedlings (which grow into large plants) require 10 to 18 inches between them, and broccoli need even more: 16 to 18 inches. Beets demand less—about 4 inches—and bunching onions, like scallions, only 2. Lettuce doesn't mind being crowded, while carrots, fighting for elbow room underground, can wind up stunted, so thin your carrot rows to at least 1 inch between plants.

As to depth, tomato plants and members of the cabbage family like to be tucked in deeper than other edibles, which, as a rule, go in as transplants at roughly the same depth they reached in pots—roots below, stems and leaves above the ground. But kale and chard seedlings, for example, want to have their root ball *and* stem buried, with just the first set of leaves showing. This thickens their stems and boosts production. Tomatoes do best if you strip off their first set of leaves and sink them up to their second set. Where the soil touches their stem, they sprout roots, and the more roots they have, the more tomatoes they'll give you. Onion bulbs, on the other hand, need only be set in ½ inch below ground, while bean plants go in at much the same depth they occupied in a pot.

Rob's cucumbers engulf more permanent mesh supports (above, left). Some beans clamber up a bed frame in the Hertz garden (above, right), while others take to teepees at Susan and Rob's (opposite).

I GROW WHATEVER I CAN VERTICALLY, ON TRELLISES, TEEPEES, FENCES, AND WALLS. ANYTHING THAT CLIMBS OR SPRAWLS IS LIKELY TO WIND UP MAKING ITS WAY SKYWARD IN MY GARDEN.

TRY A TEEPEE

If you want the flexibility to move your supports around from season to season, a bamboo teepee is a great choice. Start by using a spade to mark a circle on your soil's surface that is 2½ to 3 feet in diameter. Pound three 10-foot-long bamboo poles (at least 1½ inches thick) about 2 feet into the ground at even intervals around the circle. Pull them together at the top and secure them with heavy twine. Plant a couple of seedlings at the base of each pole, and as they grow, twine them around the pole, and if necessary, secure them with a twist tie.

THINKING VERTICALLY: GARDEN STRUCTURES

Recently, needing more space for raising seedlings, I moved my growing operation from my first pint-sized backyard to a much bigger lot closer to downtown Los Angeles. Even here, after a mere few months, my garden is, just like the last one, constantly changing. This is partly how I keep myself entertained year after year, and how I try out new varieties before passing them on to customers. Since I have so *much* to plant in such a relatively limited space, I grow whatever I can vertically, on trellises, teepees, fences, and walls. Anything that climbs or sprawls is likely to wind up making its way skyward in my garden.

To grow things vertically, you need to lay in your supports before you plant, so as not to disturb tender new roots.

Susan's husband Rob, a very resourceful guy, designed two of their four vegetable beds with permanent supports, so there's plenty of space in any season for things that ramble. When the beds were still under construction, he sank a pair of 1-inch-thick rebar rods into each bed, driving them 3 feet into the ground, with 7 feet above ground level; 5½ feet rise above the top of the garden beds. With galvanized wire, he attached a 5-by-6-foot panel of heavy-gauge, architectural wire mesh to each pair of rods, creating graceful, semi-transparent screens for plants to climb up from either side. In winter, these panels are twined with pea and sweet pea vines; in summer, with beans, cucumbers, tomatoes, and squash.

Another good vertical support is a bamboo teepee, which I used in my own first L.A. garden as the tall focal point for a bed. Bamboo poles are commonly available in garden centers. As you plant around them, observe spacing guidelines that apply to each plant.

CHAPTER

6

TENDING THE CROPS

Now that you've tucked them all in, how do you keep your edibles happy and productive while fighting off the bugs that may show up for a piece of the harvest? In this chapter, I'll answer these questions, talk a bit more about watering, and cover other vital tending tasks, including fertilizing, mulching, foliar feeding, thinning, weeding, compost tending, and pest control. While I'm at it, I hope to convince you of the pleasures and satisfactions of staying on top of routine jobs that contribute so directly to a garden's success.

City corn: Susan and Rob's crop grew up near a bougainvillea on their garage.

VERY LITTLE IN LIFE OFFERS A MORE DIRECT LINK BETWEEN EFFORT AND REWARD THAN A GARDEN.

WONDER VS. WORK

When she was little, my daughter, Porter, turned her nose up at tomatoes. Picture high summer, the Williams family gathered for dinner, and me, making a proud entrance with my platter of the fresh-picked, just-sliced harvest, still warm from the sun. Deep red, fiery orange, yellow, green, brown: I'd have them fanned out in a way I was sure no one could resist. The *smell* alone made my mouth water.

And there was Porter, her face set, mouth shut, arms crossed against any form of persuasion.

Then one summer, I gave her and Logan each garden plots. These were small, only a few feet square, and right near the back door—easy to reach, hard to forget. The deal was, they chose what they wanted to grow, and I would give them seeds and teach them some garden basics. After that, they were on their own.

Porter, who's a very visual person, made choices based on what she thought would be pretty, so among her picks was a cherry tomato.

I'm sure you see where this is going. After raising it from a seed, checking every day for the first sprout, transplanting it, watering it, lifting its leaves to look for bugs, watching it flower and then fruit, she lost her prejudice against tomatoes. It was thrilling for *me* to see this happen, and to watch her eat—and enjoy—what she had grown. I've always believed that planting a seed is one of the most spiritual of acts. Without germination, *we* wouldn't be here. It seems to me that when you taste the fruits of your labors, you understand this more deeply. It gives you, at one and the same time, a sense of awe and a sense of power. That is a big deal at any age, but especially when you're young and small.

Yet even jaded grown-ups can be moved by their influence on a garden. Forget to water, and plants droop as if hurt by your neglect. Spread organic mulch around in your beds, and you can feel with a finger how it holds heat and moisture in the soil. Foliar-feed one tomato plant and not another, and the one you feed will present you with sweeter fruit.

With each demonstration of your own impact, you may find yourself more willing to go out there and participate. This happened to me in my grandmother's garden, as it happened to Porter in mine. Gradually, as I simply did what I was told, I became part of something bigger and more mysterious than myself. Before long, no one had to give me orders. Just like Porter, I saw what needed doing and I did it.

Very little in life offers a more direct link between effort and reward than a garden. And some of the most rewarding jobs are the simplest. For instance, by just *looking* at each plant in your garden every day, you can catch problems before they escalate. If you don't, you will very likely wish you had.

A vintage watering can doubles as a garden ornament (above, left). Aztec sweet herb blooms in a bed (above, right).

ANOTHER WORD ABOUT WATERING

The first wave of edible planting falls in spring, a relatively cool, damp time compared to high summer. It makes sense that since it's often rainy then, and not yet baking hot, you'll water less early on and ramp it up as you go along. By mid-July in a dry summer, you'll be watering daily, especially thirsty vegetables like cabbage, corn, celery, and beets. Yet there are others—cucumbers, okra, and onions, for instance—that develop better if you let them dry out slightly between waterings. In Chapter 8, which covers my "must-have" plant list, you'll find plant-specific information so you can get to know what you're growing and treat it right. Rather than just dousing everything with a morning drink, you'll focus on what it needs. With the rest, a quick finger-test of the soil will tell you when it's time.

FEEDING: DON'T LET SOIL GO HUNGRY

Picture your garden's invisible life, all that goes on underground to create what you see on top. Earthworms wriggle through the soil, aerating and loosening it for better water absorption and sturdy root growth. They draw beneficial microbes, unlock nutrients for plants, and adjust soil pH to the slightly acid to neutral range edibles prefer.

The ingredients in a good organic potting mix contribute to this hidden process, as do you when you supply it, and later, when you supplement with an equally good organic fertilizer. Organic soil amendments do many things that synthetic fertilizers don't: They increase the soil's overall nutrient content, *and* they stimulate the action of worms and microbes that makes nutrients available to plants. They supply needed minerals and trace elements that chemical feeds lack. They improve soil structure and release food slowly, as plants need it. Chemicals, on the other hand, force-feed too much too fast and can harm or even kill plants. Being water soluble, they also leach out of the garden quickly, contributing to toxic runoff that damages the environment and pollutes our water supply.

If you grow your plants in organic potting soil already loaded with healthy additives, you don't need to fertilize further until a month after planting, or whenever you switch out one crop that's finished for another. You can use the HayGround fertilizer blend I've recommended (page 66), or check the Internet for a ready-mixed organic formula with similar ingredients.

When you fertilize, it's also a good idea to mulch around plants with a couple of inches of leaf mold, hay, or your own homemade compost. Mulch helps conserve moisture, even out soil temperatures, and increase microbial life as it decomposes. Since some edibles, including tomatoes, artichokes, corn, and okra, develop noticeably better if you mulch them, it's well worth the extra effort.

One of my favorite routine tasks, foliar feeding with compost tea, makes edibles sweeter and more pest resistant.

FOLIAR FEEDING: THE VEGETABLE GARDENER'S SECRET WEAPON

Here's a fact that could take your forthcoming harvest to another level: You can make any edible sweeter, more vigorous, and less vulnerable to pests and diseases by regularly spraying its leaves with compost tea or worm tea. Plants absorb more nutrients through their leaves than through their roots. And certain chewing bugs (among them, aphids and whiteflies) so dislike the smell of compost tea that they leave sprayed plants alone.

You can brew up foliar solutions yourself if you have a composter or a worm bin. Or you can turn to online sources like Gardens Alive! or Peaceful Valley Farm & Garden Supply for convenient compost-tea brewing kits, and even buy worm tea ready-made (see pages 60–1).

My own compost tea recipe is simple: Fill a galvanized bucket halfway with finished compost, top it up with water, and set it in the sun for a few days until it begins to smell a bit. Strain it, dilute it 5 parts water to 1 part tea, pour it into a spray bottle, and spray it on whole plants in the evening, including stems and the undersides of leaves.

Worm tea is even easier to make, if you have a worm bin with a spigot. Just dilute the liquid that it releases with 5 times as much water, and use as described above. Start foliar feeding with this diluted solution as soon as you plant your seedlings—or as soon as direct-sown seeds break ground—and repeat it every three weeks.

You can also use these foliar solutions either on their own or as components of the bio-stimulant mix I described on page 72, as soaking liquids to speed the germination of seeds. (Before potting them up, soak small seeds for 2 hours in the diluted tea; big, hard seeds overnight.) These same solutions can be applied to soil too, anytime, as a root feed that strengthens plants and helps them take up nutrients and ward off pests. Simply fill a watering can with diluted worm or compost tea and, when you would normally water plants, dose them generously with the solution instead.

Two friends, Lily Pearl Langos and Paul Schrade, share the work in Paul's beds.

TO THIN, OR NOT TO THIN

I've talked about carrots and similar root crops that can crowd each other underground, literally shrinking your harvest, unless you thin them when they're small. But some gardeners thin—or prune—other edibles too, especially tomatoes. The logic is that if you don't pick off a few of their flowers or their tiny, immature fruit, the fruit that ripens will be smaller and poorer.

I haven't found this to be true, and I leave the flowers and fruit alone. In fact, I notice, some always fall off on their own; the plant itself does the job for me.

But what of plants—again, the example is often tomatoes—that grow leafy and luxuriant in a way that threatens to overwhelm the fruit? Should you prune out leaves and branches to let in air and sun?

To me, this isn't necessary either, and can even be dangerous: If you over-prune tomatoes (or peppers, for that matter), leaving fruit too exposed, it's vulnerable to sunscald, which produces spots of unappetizing white or yellow skin.

What *is* critical to prune is any foliage that sweeps the ground (where it can pick up soil-borne diseases). Lifting your plant's bottom leaves improves air circulation where it counts, around its lower parts. While you're at it, nip off yellow or spotted leaves and any stems that look weak (disease attacks weak tissue).

Of course, having said these things, I encourage you to experiment, talk to friends, and see what works for you. Try thinning fruit from one plant and not another; lightly prune one and leave its neighbor alone. Trial and error hones gardening skills—and it tends to make you more observant—the most important of a gardener's tools.

WEEDING: THE NECESSARY EVIL

My grandmother called weeding "the necessary evil," and to me, it *was*—one of the few garden jobs I truly hated. I have friends who feel differently. For them, working methodically through a bed and gently routing out the chickweed, crabgrass, and oxalis serves the same meditative purpose that watering does for me.

And there are huge benefits to the garden if you stay on top of weeds, pulling or hoeing them when they're small,

since they're fast and vigorous competitors that steal water, nutrients, light, and growing space from edible plants. They can also harbor insects and diseases, not to mention that they reseed like crazy, leaving generations of themselves behind to wreak havoc on your future gardens.

One defense against weeds is something many of you already do—fill your garden beds with good-quality potting soil that isn't full of weed seeds to begin with. Raised beds have the further advantage that, being raised, they're harder for weeds to invade from the sides. In addition, planting the majority of your edible crops from seedling transplants, rather than direct-sowing seeds, gives the edibles a head start in their competition with weeds.

Whatever strategy you choose, keep an eye out every day for plants that don't belong. If you pull them out when the soil is damp (from rain or a recent watering), you'll do a better job of getting everything, roots and all.

TENDING THE COMPOST

In Chapter 4, I talked about how to start your own compost by loading grass clippings, dry leaves, and vegetable scraps, among other things, into a 3-foot-square, open-bottom bin or similarly easy-to-use container. But that's not, of course, the end of the story. You don't just start a pile and walk away—or you can, but you'll have to be very patient. It can take as much as a year for an untended batch to "finish," that is, to become the rich food called humus that so improves garden soil.

You can speed the process by "turning" compost—forking or tumbling it—which introduces oxygen and "cooks" raw materials faster. But there's an alternative to the heavy labor of turning, and I practice it myself: Once a week, I poke holes in my compost with a pole, from the top to the bottom of my bins, and then I water the holes with a hose, though not so much that water runs out visibly onto the ground. The oxygen flows in, the material is moistened, and the pile cooks more efficiently.

Since you constantly build a compost pile (with garden clippings and kitchen peelings), it's smart to have at least two, with one always further along in its decomposition than the other. This way, you'll have more ready compost on hand when you need it. As the material in your working bin (as opposed to your ready bin) breaks down and diminishes, add more of

MANY GARDENERS, ONCE THEY BEGIN TO SEE THEMSELVES AS PART OF NATURE'S CIRCLES AND CYCLES, DEVELOP A TOLERANCE FOR A CHEWED LEAF HERE AND THERE.

the same (dry leaves as well as greens, alfalfa meal, kitchen scraps, and potting soil), and top it off with a dose of compost activator, following the product's instructions. Don't worry if your green-brown ratio isn't exact, or if the pile doesn't feel hot enough. Composting is so much easier than people think. The organic matter will draw earthworms, and the earthworms will break it down, staying mostly at the edges of the bin, bottom and top, where temperatures are coolest.

If you notice your compost bin beginning to smell, it's probably too wet. Open it, poke holes with your long stick, and leave the top off so the contents can dry a bit.

WHEN IS COMPOST READY?

Anyone who doesn't believe in life after death should take a look at finished compost. It's crumbly and fluffy. It smells fresh and, well, *alive*. As a child, I couldn't get over the transformation—all the messiness of the leaves and grass, dead branches, and kitchen peelings we threw in; all the dark, sweet, crumbly stuff we shoveled out.

Here again, don't fret about getting your compost "right." If it isn't quite ready, and you need some to use, shovel aside the newest material and dig deep: You'll find more decomposed material toward the bottom of the bin. And even if you spread some on your beds that isn't quite there yet, it will draw earthworms, and they will finish the work for you.

WORM BIN TASKS

I check my worm bin every day. Is this necessary? No! But I'm an overgrown child, and I love to see those guys in there, wiggling around and making black gold for my garden! I understand that not everyone shares my enthusiasm for these busy little workers, but once you have seen them in action, and used worm tea or worm castings (their waste) on your plants, you might feel differently. In my experience, many people do!

There are several types of good worm bins, but the one I use is the Worm Factory Five-Tray Composter from Gardeners Edge (www.gardenersedge.com). Like its competitors, it comes with a detailed instruction book and everything you need to get started (except the worms, which many sources, including Peaceful Valley, carry).

As with composters, a worm bin is a pretty simple operation that allows for different approaches. It's roughly the same size as a smallish composter (perhaps 3 feet square and just as high), and it consists of several perforated plastic stacking trays with a collection tray on the bottom and a lid on top. The idea is that you fill the layers sparingly with food (for example, kitchen scraps and coffee grounds) and the worms begin at the bottom and work their way up, eating and excreting as they go.

The process begins with some peat or coir starter bedding (included with the kit) that you break up, soak in water, wring out, mix with fresh compost, and spread on dry newspaper in the lowest of several stacking trays. (The very bottom "collection" tray stays empty.) You then add a cup or so of food scraps (I use mostly greens, banana skins, coffee grounds, and a handful of alfalfa meal) to the bedding in a corner.

At this point, some people top the food with shredded newspaper before laying in the worms, then top *them* with a few sheets of damp newspaper. I skip the paper, put some worms in, cover them with a layer of potting soil, and put the lid on. You can stop there and wait for the worms to move up slowly through the holes in the trays before you fill those layers. Or, as I do, you can speed things up by loading all remaining upper trays with vegetable scraps and maybe some dry leaves or good compost, and putting a few worms in each level. They get going fast, and before you know it, the food vanishes and those former food layers are filled with castings that resemble coarse coffee grounds. These are wonderful to spread around plants or mix into container soil.

Every week, add new kitchen scraps to each layer, emptying the castings to make room. If you notice residual food in the bin that looks slimy, you're overfeeding, so cut back some. Keep your bin in a sheltered spot in the shade, and don't add any water to it, after you've soaked the starter bedding. If you live in an area of winter freezes, bring the bin inside during the cold months. In fact, you can actually keep the bin indoors year-round if you'd like—it's that tidy an operation.

My worm bins are the sort with spigots, and I put buckets fitted with strainers below these and strain the liquid as it comes out. I go a step further than some other gardeners and add 2 tablespoons of organic blackstrap molasses to each gallon of this elixir (the mineral-rich molasses is appealing to microbes and also acts as a wetting agent, helping the soon-to-be worm tea stick to plant leaves when you foliar feed). The undiluted liquid, stored in shade, keeps for up to 3 months. When I'm ready to use it, I dilute it with 5 parts water, put it in a spray bottle, and shake well.

Admittedly, some people will never warm to the idea of creating an actual home for crawling creatures that they will then have to deal with on a weekly basis—no matter how clean worms are, or how beneficial their castings. It doesn't help these gardeners to know that worm tea is higher than compost tea in micronutrients and humic acid, which is vital to a plant's nutrient uptake.

The fact is, both methods, or either one, will create miracles in your garden while helping to ease the burden we put on landfills with leftover scraps we can put to better use. This in itself is very satisfying—to recycle food to feed your garden, which, eventually, feeds you and your family.

BATTLING BUGS AND DISEASES

I have to start here by saying that *some* pest and disease problems are inevitable. By planting a garden, you're setting a beautiful table for a world of creatures, so it's no surprise that they will come. Many gardeners, once they begin to see themselves as part of nature's circles and cycles, develop a tolerance for a chewed leaf here and there, as long as it stays within certain limits. Of course, for each of us, those limits are different. Because I grow edibles commercially as well as for personal use, my standards for perfection are high, not only for my plants' health and taste but also for their appearance.

But whether you're tolerant or exacting, good gardening practices will help head off pest and disease problems. At the top of the list is growing plants in excellent, nutritious soil that makes them strong and healthy. A weak plant is a target for invasion; a well-fed plant isn't (unless you feed with chemical fertilizers, which can send plants into destructive, debilitating growing frenzies).

Also key is crop rotation, since growing plants in the same place year after year concentrates their tormentors. Beneficial companion plants can discourage tormentors, as can foliar feeding, since many insects dislike its smell. Feeding leaves fights fungus too, with beneficial bacteria. (Another fungus fighter, which also works on powdery mildew, is apple cider vinegar, diluted with 5 parts water and sprayed on leaves in the evening.) Keeping soil pathogens at a distance is a battle plan in itself, which is why I recommend growing vining plants on trellises.

Another vital weapon for gardeners is cleanliness—making sure all tools and reusable containers are scrupulously clean. A great disinfecting solution is 1 tablespoon of bleach mixed into 1 gallon of water. Use it to wash out seedling pots and trays, and dip your pruners, spades, and other tools in it at least weekly to avoid spreading any lurking diseases among your plants.

On the pest front, just being vigilant helps keep them in check—go out every day on patrol and examine the soil and all leaf surfaces, including undersides, where bugs often gravitate. Certain pests are easily controlled with hand picking. I gather root-eating grubs in pans for the neighborhood birds. Friends of mine feed marauding slugs to their chickens. Eventually, though, other bugs get out of hand, and that's where organic controls come in. You certainly don't want to kill the good guys along with the bad, and there are plenty of good guys in a well-tended organic garden.

A busy bee gathers pollen from flowering dandelion greens.

Natural Pest Control by Andrew Lopez is one of the best references I know on this complicated subject, and it presents a system of integrated management that includes choosing pest-resistant plant varieties (where available and desirable), watchfulness, hand picking, effective fertilizing and watering, the use of beneficial insects, and natural insecticides.

As I'm hinting here, pest-resistant varieties, bred or selected primarily *for* such resistance, are often much less flavorful than the heirlooms we grow because they remind us of how food used to taste. Why bother with bland tomatoes? I'd rather use beneficial insects, companion plants, and organic insecticide as part of my overall garden program and have *great* tomatoes—and peppers, eggplants, and squash!

Many catalogs, such as Peaceful Valley and Gardens Alive!, offer a range of beneficial insects: ladybugs, which go after aphids; lacewings, whose targets include mealybugs, caterpillars, aphids, and thrips; certain mini-wasps that devour flies; and insect parasitic nematodes that eat the larvae of pests that live in soil.

The range of organic insecticides is even broader. BT *(Bacillus thuringiensis),* for example, a naturally occurring bacteria, controls the cutworms that ravage many edibles. Milky spores, another bacterial insecticide, take aim at grubs, especially the Japanese beetle grub. Diatomaceous earth—the ground, fossilized shells of small, aquatic animals—creates a sharp barrier against slugs and snails. Concentrated garlic extracts ward off sucking insects; insecticidal soap (made from potassium salts) kills other leaf eaters, including aphids and grasshoppers; hot pepper wax gets these as well, along with whiteflies and spider mites. Pyola (derived from chrysanthemums and canola oil) takes care of a host of bad bugs (aphids, beetles, and caterpillars, for instance), but it will snuff some good ones too unless you're careful and spot-spray it.

The point is, you have a wide variety of weapons to choose from in trying to keep pest and disease problems within *your* acceptable limits. But remember that good gardening is really the best defense—that and spending time *in* your garden, paying attention to all the little things that, together, contribute to the health of the community you're creating.

JUST BEING VIGILANT HELPS KEEP PESTS IN CHECK—GO OUT EVERY DAY ON PATROL AND EXAMINE THE SOIL AND ALL LEAF SURFACES, INCLUDING THE UNDERSIDES, WHERE BUGS OFTEN GRAVITATE.

Japanese cucumbers ramble up a teepee in Sarajo Frieden's garden.

CHAPTER

7

BRINGING IN THE BEANS

Within a few short weeks, your fledgling crops do go, literally, from seed to skillet. By now, you will have had a front-row seat as your radishes have broken ground, grown up, and asked, with their round, red shoulders, to be picked. Vines will have reached out tendrils, formed pods, and revealed their swelling peas. It's easy to see when a lettuce or tomato is ready to eat, harder with an underground potato. But there are signals if you know how to look. In this chapter, I'll focus on the harvest and what to do as particular plants run their course. I'm going to talk about seed saving, soil renewal, and, for those of you in cold climates, how to put your garden to bed for the winter. Planning, preparation, and timing are everything in a garden, but let's not forget to enjoy the harvest!

HARES AND TORTOISES

A radish goes from seed to table in less than a month. A winter squash or 'Black Brandywine' tomato can take four times as long. Planting seedlings instead of seeds does speed the process considerably, but this won't change the fact that some crops reward you almost instantly, while others reward you for being patient. Each is satisfying in its own way: Given the hard work of starting a garden, it's great to get results fast; in fact, it can seem almost miraculous. At the same time, almost nothing is as sweet as the tomato you've watched and waited for throughout the summer, or the squash you pick in September, tuck away, and bake into a spicy bread during winter.

The average wait for a crop harvest tends to fall somewhere between these two poles, and it requires you to watch your plants. It's easy to confuse the first slim string beans with a bean plant's stems, or to miss tender young zucchini amid a riot of foliage. But that bean plant, which produces more the more you pick it, will stop producing altogether if you don't. And we all know about the bat-sized zucchini that seem to arrive suddenly from nowhere, too big for good eating.

KEEPING AN EYE OUT

With most edibles, knowing when to harvest is as simple as looking closely. Most develop and fruit where you can see it, and if you're not sure the moment is right, you can always pick one and taste it. You can also do this with root crops, which are harder to judge but may have their own ways of tipping you off: potato foliage, for example, often dies off when potatoes are ready to dig. In Chapter 8, where I give cultivation tips for individual plants, you'll find more information on harvesting in cases where it isn't obvious.

If you're not expecting it, you might be surprised at how much even a small plot, when managed well, produces— enough for your own needs, very likely, as well as gift baskets for friends, food banks, and homeless shelters. Being able to share the bounty with others deepens the pleasure even more of having grown it yourself.

WEIGHING THE OPTIONS

Naturally, harvest times, especially those that finish off a particular crop, present opportunities and demand decisions. What's next for that picked-clean cabbage or carrot patch? How do you choose one crop to succeed another, and then prepare the ground to receive it?

For me, the best answer for "What's next?" is always, "What would you like to eat?" If you've still got enough time in the summer season, and you *haven't* had enough carrots, there's nothing wrong with planting them again, in exactly the same place, since they won't be there terribly long. What you don't want to do is locate the same thing in the same spot

A summer dinner in John and Diane Hertz's vegetable garden (opposite). The harvest approaches (below, left to right): 'Ronde de Nice' zucchini, haricots verts, a baby cucumber, and tomatoes ripening on the vine.

SAVING EGGPLANT SEEDS

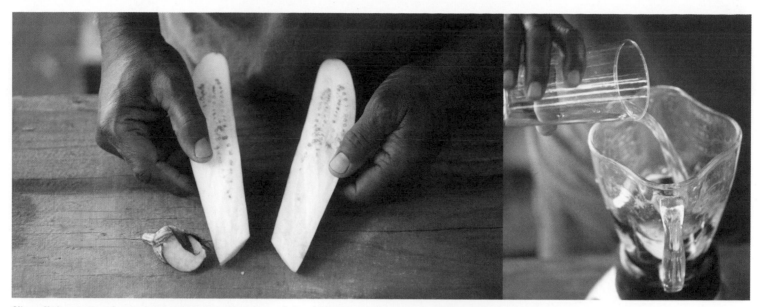

Slice off the stem end, cut the eggplant in half, and toss it in a blender with 2 cups of purified water.

Blend for about 30 seconds to release the seeds, then strain the liquid from the pulp.

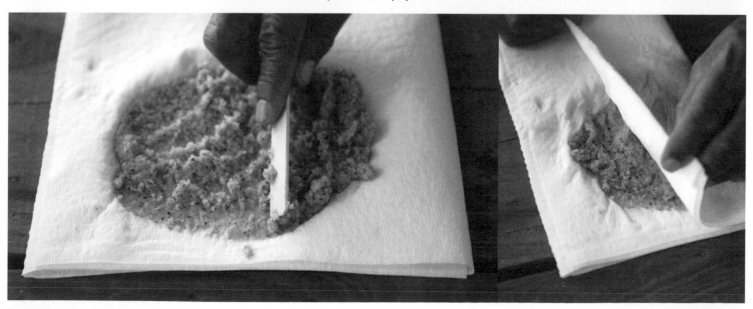

Spread the pulp on paper towels, fold the towels and store in a well-ventilated place away from direct sunlight for about 2 or 3 days until seeds are dry and ready to plant.

IF YOU'RE NOT EXPECTING IT, YOU MIGHT BE SURPRISED AT HOW MUCH EVEN A SMALL PLOT, WHEN MANAGED WELL, PRODUCES. . . .

In Los Angeles, summer's rewards include sprightly feverfew blooms (above); fruiting passionflowers (below, left), and lettuces-to-go (below, right).

'Bright Lights' Swiss chard (above, left), 'Red Russian' kale (above, right).

year after year, which encourages pest build-up. Within a single season, though, you're safe if you refresh the soil between crops with nutrients depleted by the first one. For carrots and other root vegetables, bonemeal does the job in combination with my HayGround fertilizer blend and your own homemade compost. For a typical 6-foot carrot row, between harvesting and replanting, dig into the soil 3 cups of bonemeal, 1 cup of my HayGround fertilizer blend, and 2 to 3 inches of compost, then plant as you did the first time around. When you plant next *spring,* on the other hand, you should relocate your carrots to a different spot.

GIVERS AND TAKERS

If you're changing out crops within a single season, something else to consider is which plants like to follow others. I touched on this in Chapter 5—the fact that some, like peas and beans, fix nitrogen in the soil, so it's smart to succeed them, whenever possible, with nitrogen-hungry plants. For instance, when your peas have run their course, swap in lettuce or other greens. (Remember, though, in mid-summer, to choose heat-tolerant lettuce varieties and shelter them in a bed with taller plants.) Even in this case, you'll need to amend your soil, leaving out the bonemeal recommended for the carrots but working 3 cups of my HayGround fertilizer blend into every 6-foot lettuce row, along with 2 to 3 inches of organic compost.

As you clean out beds, if you plan to save seed, you won't yank every spent plant but let a couple of them flower. After a few weeks, many put on quite a show, sending stems up several feet and erupting in cornflower blues (dandelion greens), creamy whites (arugula), and mustard golds (lettuce). (For more seed-saving information, see the cultivation notes on specific plants in Chapter 8.)

During summer's dog days, it can be hard to imagine autumn, not that many of us want to. But in cool climates, mid-summer is the time to plant fall crops like turnips, kale, chard, and spinach, if you want to enjoy them before winter. These can sub in, say, for early determinate tomatoes (those that ripen all at once rather than continuing to produce), bolted lettuce, or peas, and the amending process is the same: for root crops, add bonemeal, fertilizer, and compost; for others, skip the bonemeal and up the fertilizer and compost. (In mild winter climates, you would do this toward the end of summer.)

TUCKING UP FOR WINTER

I used to cherish the solemn ritual of putting the garden to bed for the winter, the part of the cycle that signaled an end to something rich and memorable but contained a promise for the future season of rebirth—spring, my *favorite* season. As the cold came on, we Williams children forgot our August laziness and sprang into action, pulling the dried stalks and vines from the beds so they couldn't serve as a winter breeding ground for pests and diseases. We worked fertilizer into the empty beds, topped them with a few inches of finished compost, then piled on 6 inches of dry leaves to keep the beds warm for the worms. All the plant debris from summer went back into the emptied compost to cook until April. I often thought about that—all the action underground, the busy life beneath the snow, the legions of earthworms that awaited us when everything began again.

If your climate prevents you from winter growing, it's wise to clear, enrich, and cover your beds in the way I've described above. After taking out plants, dig in 6 cups of my HayGround fertilizer blend and a 3-inch topping of compost per each 4-by-6-foot bed. If you've got a supply of dry leaves, work those in too and cover with more, or else mulch thickly with hay or top with black plastic. The worms *will* stick around, and come spring, you'll start the next garden season with super soil, endowed, as I always saw it in my childish mind, with super powers to grow amazing food for the people you love.

Cherry tomatoes ripen on the vine in Jonathan Berg and Dede Gardner-Berg's raised beds.

FROM SEED TO SKILLET

ALMOST NOTHING IS AS SWEET AS THE TOMATO YOU'VE WATCHED AND WAITED FOR THROUGHOUT THE SUMMER, OR THE SQUASH YOU PICK IN SEPTEMBER, TUCK AWAY, AND BAKE INTO A SPICY BREAD DURING WINTER.

In Susan and Rob's garden, golden flowers (below, left) develop into Kabocha squash, which climbs a trellis (below, right).

·CHAPTER·

8

THE EDIBLE A-LIST OF MUST-HAVE VEGETABLES, HERBS, AND FRUIT

In this chapter, I'll get specific about good things to grow and what each needs to produce well. I've covered general guidelines for edibles, how and when to water, how to ward off pests, how to cook up compost and worm tea. I've said that foliar feeding will make all plants stronger and your harvest sweeter. Now, here's the word on which vegetables prefer even moisture and which like to dry out between waterings; which want to be deeply planted or widely spaced; which grow best shallowly and in crowds. Because cultivation differences among plants affect your success with them, I encourage you to learn the specifics for those you grow. This kind of knowledge is another tool for your collection, and one of the most important. Finally, I will list some of my favorite varieties for each edible group—the ones I know and have grown with great results.

ARTICHOKES

These plants thrive in the mild climates of Northern and Southern California, where they're grown as perennials, often as much for their ornamental silver-blue foliage as for their thistly heads, which are transformed by steaming into a tender delicacy. In Los Angeles, we can expect two crops a year—in spring and in autumn. In colder regions, people tend the plants through summer for a fall harvest, with the most ambitious gardeners pulling up and over-wintering their roots as you would with tender flower bulbs.

You can start seeds indoors in pots in late winter, transplanting the larger, greener seedlings about 8 weeks later, or when frost danger has passed and soil is at least 55 degrees. (Ideal soil pH is 6.0 to 6.8.) Since artichokes (*Cynara scolymus*) are big plants, space them 3 to 6 feet apart, and feed each with a cup of my HayGround fertilizer blend or a shovelful of composted chicken manure. (If you're planting in a raised bed full of fresh, top-grade potting soil, wait 3 weeks to fertilize.) Keep plants evenly moist, never letting soil dry out completely, and control snails and slugs with an organic product such as Sluggo.

If you see ants gravitating toward the center of plants, the artichokes probably have scale, which you can head off with targeted doses of Pyola.

Harvest flower heads just before they bloom. Since these plants don't normally come true from seed, the best propagation method, if you want to replicate the plants you have, is to harvest the small, rooted "pups" from the base of older artichokes and plant them out separately.

MY TOP PICKS
'Purple Romagna', 'Green Globe', 'Violetto', 'Imperial Star'

ASPARAGUS

Grown by the Greeks and Romans and increasingly popular today as one of the first great vegetables of spring, asparagus puts off some gardeners because it demands a substantial commitment of space and takes 3 to 4 years to produce from seed. While the dedicated area (at least 4 by 4 feet to grow enough for two people) is a problem for urbanites on small lots, there is a way to get a crop faster—by planting "crowns." These 2- to 3-year-old tentacled roots, sold by mail-order nurseries, produce plants and spears in one season. If you let these die back instead of cutting them, your *next* year's crop will be a good one. You *can* grow *Asparagus officinalis* in a large (2-foot-deep) pot, but it might not yield enough to make you happy.

The secret to success with asparagus is first to order your crowns from a reputable source (see "Top Seed and Seedling Sources," page 60) so they will be free from the fusarium wilt that can plague this plant. Even before ordering, contact your Cooperative Extension office for a list of varieties that work best in your area. Once crowns arrive, plant them quickly (as long as frost danger has passed), in soil with a pH between 6.0 and 7.0, after digging your bed deeply and adding lots of organic matter.

Choose a spot in full sun, and spade and loosen the soil thoroughly, picking out weeds and working in generous amounts of leaf mold (4 bags per 4-by-6-foot bed). Before tucking in the crowns, add 1 to 2 cups of my HayGround fertilizer blend per plant. Then, dig a trench 6 to 12 inches deep (deeper in cold climates), add a few inches of compost, and arrange the crowns on compost mounds 10 to 15 inches apart. Cover with more soil, and continue to fill in the trench as the shoots grow through. When you've filled in to ground level, top the bed with a layer of organic mulch.

During the first season, water consistently, about an inch a week (which, according to a common rule of thumb, amounts to a bit more than ½ gallon total for a plant in 1 square foot of soil). Don't let your bed dry out. (You will water less in subsequent seasons.) Wait until the year after planting to harvest, snapping or cutting spears that are pencil-sized or larger. Stop harvesting when spears diminish in diameter to pencil-size only, and feed the bed with my HayGround fertilizer blend (2 cups per 4-by-6-foot bed). After the remaining spears grow big and bushy and eventually yellow, cut them to the ground and throw them away (not in your compost pile in case they are diseased). Cover the bed with a couple of inches of compost in the fall, and fertilize again, as above, in early spring.

If slugs and snails show up about that time, hand pick, or apply an organic product such as Sluggo Plus. Control asparagus beetles with targeted doses of Pyola.

After 2 or 3 years of harvests, you will get larger spears if you divide your plants, digging up the roots, breaking them apart, and replanting every 6 to 8 inches. This is also a way to propagate asparagus, or share it with gardening friends.

MY TOP PICKS
'Mary Washington', 'Purple Passion'

THE BEAN FAMILY

"Generous" is a word that comes to mind when I think about beans. In so many ways, these plants are givers. They produce copious amounts of food, even when grown in containers. They add nitrogen to the soil, essentially feeding heavy nitrogen consumers, such as corn, that follow them in a planting bed. Pole and bush beans *(Phaseolus vulgaris)* can be eaten in any of three stages—as green pods, freshly shelled seeds, or dried beans. Fava beans *(Vicia faba)* are beautiful, edible plants with dainty flowers and intriguing, upward-growing pods that extend the whole bean season—since they are cool growers you plant in late winter, even before frost ends. Lima beans *(Phaseolus lunatus),* which most people know in dry, bagged form from supermarkets, are a treat when picked early, before they harden on the vine, and simmered or sautéed in olive oil.

Whichever bean(s) you grow, here are some tips for success: Beans prefer well-drained soil with a pH above 6.0. Most beans want warm (70- to 90-degree) soil, while favas germinate at cooler temps. Be sure the seeds you plant are fresh. Bean seeds are viable for a year or two at most. Use an inoculant at planting time. A type of beneficial bacteria sold by Peaceful Valley, Seedway.com, and other online sources, an inoculant enables the plant to capture nitrogen from the air and fix it in the soil. It increases the plant's disease-resistance, sturdiness, and yield. Applying it is simple. Begin by watering your indoor starter pot or garden bed lightly. Make a 1-inch-deep hole for each seed, drop it in, put a pinch of inoculant on top, and cover with soil.

For pole beans, which you space 2 inches apart, add the pole or other structure at planting time so as not to disturb roots later. Space bush beans 18 inches apart. Let plants dry out some between waterings, and keep an eye out for Mexican bean beetles, which you can control with targeted applications of Pyola.

Harvest beans regularly to keep them productive. (Surprisingly, this can be a challenge, especially for beans like fine French *haricots verts,* which can so resemble plant stems that it's hard to tell the difference.)

Different bean varieties can be cross-pollinated by bees, so William Woys Weaver, author of *Heirloom Vegetable Gardening*, recommends planting flowers nearby to divert the bees. To save seeds, let the beans dry on the plant, then shake the dry plants into a bag to release the seeds. To keep bean weevils from eating the seeds, add a pinch of diatomaceous earth to your storage jar or packet and shake to coat the seeds.

MY TOP PICKS

'Fin de Bagol', 'Black Valentine', 'Brittle Yellow Wax', 'French Pole', 'Royalty Purple Pod', 'Empress Green', 'Gold of Bacau', 'Weezy's Butterbean', 'Dixie Speckled Butterpea', 'Chinese Red Noodle', 'Peach Runner', 'Scarlet Runner', 'Neckargold', 'Cupidon', 'Peruvian Purple' favas

THE BEET FAMILY (BEETS AND CHARD)

Both singled out for their health value in a 1942 *Victory Gardens* pamphlet, beets and chard are not only good for you, they're also culinary workhorses. Different forms of the same plant (*Beta vulgaris),* beets are grown mainly for their bulbous roots, and chards for their leaves, though to me, beet greens are every bit as delicious as chard. I use them interchangeably in soups and stews, and in any Southern dish that calls generically for "greens." Chard is a leaf crop only, but so generous and long lasting, that once you grow it, you'll wonder how you did without it.

All forms of *Beta vulgaris* share similar cultivation needs. They prefer moist, light soil with a pH between 6.0 and 7.0 and cool, even temperatures. (Dramatic weather shifts may cause "zoning," the formation of tough rings in beets.)

I generally plant them in winter for a spring harvest and again in summer to pick in fall. Cool-zone gardeners can start seeds in cold frames or indoor trays (¼ inch deep, 3 to 4 seeds per inch of soil) 5 or 6 weeks before the last average frost date. Because their seeds have very hard shells, as I noted in Chapter 4, they need prepping before sowing. When my grandmother cracked them first with a rolling pin, they sprouted twice as fast as uncracked ones. Or, you can soak the seeds overnight in my bio-stimulant recipe (page 72) to boost the speed, health, disease-resistance, and yield of your crops.

For planting out, when heavy-frost danger has passed, prepare the soil in your garden bed as you do for carrots, digging and loosening it 12 to 16 inches deep and adding 1 cup of bonemeal per 4-foot row of plants. Lay out seedlings 4 inches apart, burying each one in the ground about ½ inch up the stem, or plant at the same depth in a large container.

Don't let the soil dry out. I'm not saying it should be boggy—just slightly moist to the touch. Among other things, this will prevent beet scab, which disfigures roots with rough brown patches. If you have particularly alkaline soil, you can also feed plants with boron (a mineral available from many online sources, including Peaceful Valley), following product directions.

Unfortunately, snails and slugs love beets and chard as much as I do, so be vigilant about picking them off, and/or applying a good organic repellant like Sluggo Plus as needed.

As to seed saving, these plants are biennial, so cold-climate gardeners must lift and overwinter them. This involves tucking them in a moist, cool medium (such as sand) and storing them in a cellar, before planting them out and letting them bolt and bloom in spring. Here, I leave them in the garden bed until they flower and go to seed. Then, as with many seed heads, I usually hang them, bagged, upside-down to dry, and the seeds come loose easily for putting aside and replanting.

MY TOP PICKS

Beets: 'Chioggia', 'Bull's Blood', 'Yellow Cylindrical', 'Crosby's Egyptian', 'Mammoth Red Mangel', 'Touchstone Gold', 'Blankoma', 'Golden Eckendorf', 'Lutz Green Leaf', 'Forono', 'McGregor's Favorite'
Chard: 'San Francisco', 'Five-Color Silverbeet' (Rainbow), 'Canary Yellow', 'Flamingo Pink', 'Oriole Orange', 'Vulcan'

BLUEBERRIES

Lately, I've found, I can hardly keep up with the demand for blueberry plants—both from my design clients and my farmers' market customers. These berries' (well-deserved) reputation for nutritional value is one reason, and another is that more and more low-chill varieties, suitable for growing in mild regions like Los Angeles, are being grown for sale. A third is the fresh-taste factor. There's just no comparison between a store-bought clamshell of blueberries (known botanically as *Vaccinium*) and ones you pick and eat from a bush at home. And what a robust, pretty bush! It flowers white in spring, its foliage reddens in fall, and its fruit erupts in colorful waves, from green to pinky-red to deep blue, that can all deck out a bush at once. The plants live for years and years, unlike most other edibles, which come and go in a flash. In fact, blueberries aren't fully mature until they've been in the ground for 4 to 6 seasons.

To choose plants that are right for you, you need to know your USDA Climate Zone (I talked about this in Chapter 3) and the chilling requirements of different blueberry varieties. In order to set fruit, most need 150 to 800 hours annually of temperatures below 45 degrees, but others will produce with much less. Your local County Extension office can recommend varieties suitable for your climate, and you can also find online sources and information.

Blueberries grow best in full sun, in moist but well-drained soil with a pH between 3.5 and 5.5—much more acidic than most other edibles in your garden. (One way to bring down your soil pH is to amend the bed with large amounts of organic matter like shredded bark and/or well-composted leaves, along with organic garden sulfur.) Either online or from a local nursery, buy 2- or 3-year-old shrubs (they usually come bare-root through the mail) and plant them in spring in cooler zones, in spring or autumn in mild climates. If you grow more than one variety, you'll likely get more fruit, thanks to cross-pollination, an advantage here, where your goal is to increase the crop rather than collect and save a single type of seed. Space plants 4 to 6 feet apart; half that if you're creating a berry hedge. Or plant dwarf varieties in very large, deep pots. Keep them well watered, and fertilize as they begin to bloom, with 1 cup per plant of an organic fertilizer formulated for acid-loving plants. Repeat this application 3 to 4 times a year in mild climates, and every spring and fall in cold-winter zones. As with raspberries, once fruit appears, you'll probably want to net your shrubs to ward off hungry birds.

MY TOP PICKS
'O'Neal', 'Misty', 'South Moon', 'Sharpe Blue', 'Ozark Blue', 'Bluecrop', 'Spartan'

THE CABBAGE FAMILY

For thousands of years, we human beings have relished the nutritious members of the cabbage clan, from wild, leafy Mediterranean natives to the tighter, head-forming types first cultivated in Northern Europe. Over time, in different climates and cultures, farmers selectively bred for particular qualities of these plants, and distinctive subgroups were born: large-leafed kale; small, round-leafed collards; turnip-like kohlrabi; crinkly savoys and other head cabbage; as well as broccoli, cauliflower, and Brussels sprouts. All belong to the species *Brassica oleracea* and share many cultivation needs.

They like cool temperatures, moist soil, a pH range from 5.0 (the low end for broccoli) to 7.5 (the high end for kohlrabi), and plenty of sun. While gardeners in very mild regions like mine may plant them first in late winter and again as summer wanes (for a fall harvest), those in harsher climates often settle for one crop per year. They're easy to grow. In fact, cabbage, kale, and collards will even produce in pots.

For garden growing, start seeds indoors in a bright room about 6 weeks before your area's average last frost date. Plant ¼ inch deep and 1 to 2 inches apart in pots or flats, and watch for germination in 5 to 17 days. Once the threat of hard frost has passed, you can plant out seedlings that have at least 6 leaves (or equally developed purchased seedlings), burying 1 inch of each plant's stem and leaving 16 to 18 inches between plants in a raised bed full of good-quality potting soil. Alternatively, if you're planting in unamended flat ground, dig 1½ to 2 cups of blended organic fertilizer around each plant. (In a raised bed, do the same thing 3 weeks after transplanting.)

Watch for pests, especially cabbage worm, which you can prevent with applications of BT, even up to the day of harvest. Also, keep an eye out for maturing crops; as spring and summer heat up, they come on fast, forming tight heads that will split if left unpicked, or, in the case of broccoli and cauliflower, begin to splay. Cut the fattened stems of kohlrabi (its "bulbs") when they're 2 to 3 inches thick. For kale, pick outer leaves first; the plant will continue sprouting new leaves at its center. Collards, which tolerate heat *and* cold better than their cabbage kin, will keep leafing out into late autumn if you harvest tender foliage from the bottom of the stalk upward.

To save seed, let plants flower and produce pods, and when these begin to turn brown, cut their stems, bag their heads, and thrash them to release the seed.

MY TOP PICKS
Broccoli: 'Umpqua', 'Small Miracle', 'Romanesco', 'De Cicco', 'Green Goliath', 'Calabrese Green Sprouting', 'Early Purple Sprouting', 'Purple Peacock' **Brussels sprouts:** 'Red Rubine', 'Evesham Special', 'Catskill' **Cabbage:** 'January King', 'Filderkraut', 'Glory of Enkhuizen', 'Charleston Wakefield', 'Melissa' and 'Drumhead' (both savoys) **Cauliflower:** 'Maystar', 'Purple Cape', 'Galleon', 'Early Snowball', 'Brocoverde' **Collards:** tree collards, 'Georgia Southern', 'Morris Heading' **Kale:** Appalachian wild napus, 'Black Tuscan' palm tree, 'Ragged Jack', 'White Russian', 'Red Chidori' **Kohlrabi:** 'Purple Vienna', 'Superschmelz', 'Dyna Purple', 'Kossak Giant'

CARROTS

With their delicate, ferny foliage, which smells appealingly like the root itself, carrots are among the prettiest of homegrown vegetables. They're rewarding plants too: As I watch them sprout and grow tall, imagining what's taking shape underground, I feel I'm in on one of the earth's great secrets. I'm constantly out checking them—looking for the telltale "shoulders" that appear at the base of the stems as they develop.

We know that the Romans appreciated the carrot, *Daucus carota,* both as a food and as a medicine (reportedly, even as an aphrodisiac). Dutch settlers and English colonists brought it to North America, where Pilgrims grew it, and Native Americans adopted it enthusiastically. Why not? Carrots are delicious and healthy, full of nutrients like vitamin C and potassium, and the antioxidant beta-carotene, which is great for vision.

And there are so many carrots to choose from! Their colors range from yellow and purple to vivid red-orange; their shapes from fetching little balls and short, chubby cylinders to long tapers ('Japanese Imperial Long' can reach 3 feet!).

Carrots will grow in cool or warm conditions, but you'll harvest the best ones before the full blast of summer heat. If you prefer starting seedlings indoors, plant seeds ¼ inch deep and as little as ½ inch apart 6 weeks before your average last frost date. When they're a couple of inches tall—and hard-frost danger has passed—they're ready to move outside.

But this is a crop you can easily direct-sow in the garden, if you prepare the ground first. Spading your bed in advance (12 to 16 inches down) is critical for carrots to develop fully, whether you direct-sow seeds or plant seedlings. They like a soil pH of about 6.5, and they need scant nitrogen, so once you've dug the bed, add only 1 cup of bonemeal (excellent for root vegetables) and 2 hefty shovelfuls of compost per 4-foot row, and work it all in. Except for regular foliar feeding (every 3 weeks or so), you won't need to fertilize again.

To direct-sow, make a furrow with your finger (about ¼ inch deep) down your bed and line it sparingly with seeds. Remember, you're going to thin the plants that sprout, to between 1 and 4 inches apart, so if you lay down too many, you'll be thinning forever. Use the same spacing if you plant seedlings, immersing each plant in the ground up to its lowest set of leaves. You can also raise carrots in containers.

Let your crop dry out slightly between waterings (put your finger down an inch to test the soil), and watch for pests: The carrot fly maggot (this plant's nemesis) can be controlled, if and when it appears, with targeted applications of Pyola. To head off root knot nematode, which deforms carrots, plant marigolds or garlic as their companions.

Carrots are biennial and need a few weeks of cold to flower. In mild climates like mine, you can leave a few in the ground until they go to seed, then cut the plants and hang them upside down, either bagged or set above a cloth to catch the seeds for future crops. In cold-winter regions, harvest some of your carrot favorites in autumn, snip the tops, leaving a couple of inches of root, and store in a damp, cool (between 35- and 40-degree) place. Plant them out in the spring a good 2 feet apart with their "shoulders" buried, and let them grow and go to seed.

MY TOP PICKS

'Rodelika', 'Yellowstone', 'Purple Haze', 'Red Samurai', 'Nantaise', 'Cosmic Purple', 'Royal Chantenay', 'Little Finger', 'Napoli', 'Parmex', 'Kinko'

CELERY

You might not think to plant celery *(Apium graveolens),* which is available year-round in grocery stores and has a reputation for being somewhat touchy in the garden. But common stem varieties, arguably the hardest to grow, are only one of the forms this vegetable takes. There's also a leaf, or cutting, variety—as easy to raise as parsley (even in a pot), and full of concentrated celery flavor—that you can snip for soups and salads. A third option is the root variety, celeriac, probably most familiar julienned and tossed with rémoulade. All are worth trying at least once, and as you come to understand their needs, you might decide to stick with them.

Celery loves water and rich soil (with a pH between 6.5 and 7.5), amended with lots of organic matter. It doesn't like summer heat, so in cool climates, start it in early spring for fall harvest, and in hot places, in fall for spring picking. You can start it indoors, planting seeds ¼ inch deep and 2 inches apart and transplanting seedlings to the garden when soil temps are at least 65 degrees. Space them a foot apart and spread 1½ to 2 cups of my HayGround fertilizer blend

around each, then foliar feed 3 weeks later and at 3-week intervals thereafter.

Keep your celery bed moist and watch its development, being careful to harvest before the stalks—or roots—have toughened. In the case of leaf celery, the more you snip, the more it grows. Foliar feeding helps hold off aphids, but if they show up for a taste, blast them with a hose, a squirt of pepper oil, or a targeted application of Pyola.

The three celery types will cross-pollinate if you grow them near each other. If you want to save seeds, the biennial stem and root forms must be over-wintered, planted out again in spring, and allowed to flower and go to seed.

MY TOP PICKS

Celery root: 'Brilliant' **Leaf celery:** 'French Dinant', 'Zwolsche Krul'
Stem celery: 'Giant Red', 'Yellow Beauty', 'Utah', 'Conquistador'

CORN

CUCUMBERS

Known botanically as *Zea mays,* corn is a nitrogen-loving plant, so it's a good one to locate in a bed where you've last grown peas or beans. You *can* start it indoors, but since it's touchy about root disturbance, sow seeds in a plug tray or 6-pack, which will enable you to pop out seedlings with a gentle squeeze. You can also direct-sow seeds right into your beds, after first spreading 2 to 3 inches of compost on top and working it in. Plant seeds in a furrow 1 to 2 inches deep and 2 inches apart, but be ready to thin seedlings as they develop, to about 18 inches apart. Because corn is wind pollinated, you'll need at least 4 rows to get a good yield. In soil with a pH between 5.5 and 6.8 and a minimum temperature of 65 degrees, seeds germinate fast. When sprouts reach 4 to 6 inches tall (or at transplant time, if you've pregrown or bought seedlings), spread ½ cup of my HayGround fertilizer blend around each plant and mix it into the soil.

Water plants consistently and well, as often as daily in summer heat, never allowing them to dry out. Watch for worms, especially cutworms, and control them with BT.

Corn varieties growing within 2 miles of one another cross-pollinate easily, so it's hard to ensure the purity of your seed. If you'd like to save the seed anyway and see what you get, let the kernels dry on the cobs on the plant, then remove and store them until you need them. (Adding a pinch of diatomaceous earth, available through mail-order sources, to your packet of seeds and shaking to coat them will protect them from weevils.)

MY TOP PICKS
'Golden Bantam Sweet', 'Country Gentleman', 'Hopi Blue', 'Cherokee White Eagle', 'Black Aztec'

Homegrown cucumbers are thinner-skinned, less watery, and sweet, a rewarding summer crop that will do fine in a large container. There are many heirlooms to choose from, including small pickling types and larger ones, such as 'Improved Long Green'.

A native of India, *Cucumis sativus* takes bush and vining forms, and the vines need a trellis or other structure to climb on. Germination is fast (4 to 13 days in soil at least 65 degrees, with a pH of about 6.5), but if you start seeds indoors in pots, you must plant them out no more than 3 weeks later.

Before sowing seeds, fill your container to 1 inch below the rim with good potting soil, then add ½ cup of my HayGround fertilizer blend, cover with more potting soil, and plant seeds ½ inch deep. (Take care not to get fertilizer *on* seeds, which will cause them to rot.)

Set transplants (or seedlings you buy) out in beds ½ inch deep and 3 feet apart for bush varieties; 6 inches for vining types. Let them dry out slightly between waterings, and foliar feed, as with all edibles, at 3-week intervals to increase sugar. Control cucumber beetles with spot applications of Pyola.

Save seeds by letting a couple of cukes grow large and a little mushy before picking, then removing the seeds, cleaning them, and letting them dry in cool shade. You won't necessarily get the same plants next year, since cukes are easily cross-pollinated by roving bees.

MY TOP PICKS
'Richmond Green Apple', 'Chinese Yellow', 'Boothby's Blond', 'Uzbekski', 'Early Russian', 'Black Diamond', 'Poona Kheera', 'West Indian Burr Gherkin', 'Delikatesse', 'Diva'

EGGPLANT

One of the best things about living in an increasingly multi-cultural country is how freely we borrow from one another's food traditions. Many of my friends and clients who didn't grow up eating eggplant now count *Solanum melongena* among their favorite vegetables, having first tasted it in Asian, Greek, or Italian restaurants. William Woys Weaver, in his book *Heirloom Vegetable Gardening,* calls eggplants "creatures of the tropics," for their partiality to hot days and nights, and he also points out the many new varieties that have appeared in the United States from Africa and Asia. As gardeners, we can take advantage of these exotics, which rarely make it to the supermarket. Even those with little outdoor space can grow them—in pots.

If you grow from seed, you'll get a bigger payoff in healthier plants if you coddle these just a bit. Start seeds indoors at least 3 weeks before your last predicted frost, planting ¼ inch deep. When seedlings develop their second leaf set, transplant each to a larger pot. By the time it's warm enough to plant them outside, they'll have a stronger, more extensive root system.

In the garden bed, where they favor soil temps between 75 and 90 degrees and a pH of about 6.5, space them 10 to 18 inches apart and apply ½ cup of my HayGround fertilizer blend around each plant. (If your bed is raised and full of fresh, top-grade potting soil, wait a month to fertilize.) Spreading a couple of inches of organic mulch—hay or leaf mold, for example—in the eggplant bed will help the soil hold heat.

Let the soil dry somewhat between waterings, and keep an eye out for drooping foliage in plants that *aren't* in need of water. This could signal verticillium or fusarium wilt, conditions eggplant is susceptible to, and for which the only solution is to yank and throw away the plant (*not* in your compost, where the wilt will spread and wreak larger garden havoc). Control whatever moths or worms show up with BT.

Seed saving is a snap, despite the small size of eggplant seeds: Put seed-containing pulp in a blender with purified water and puree; strain the mixture to separate out the seeds; drain thoroughly in paper towels; and the seeds are ready to plant—without soaking. (You can also store them in a cool place for the future.) See "Saving Eggplant Seeds," page 110.

MY TOP PICKS
'Striped Toga', 'Rosita', 'Thai Green Pea', 'Udumalapet', 'Apple Green', 'Goyo Kumba', 'Ping Tung Long', 'Lao Purple Stripe', 'African Purple', 'Thai Yellow Egg'

HERBS

The list of herbs that I think I can't live without gets longer by the year. Basil is right there near the top, of course, as the perfect bedmate *and* flavor partner for tomatoes; thyme is a must-have for soups and stews (not to mention the Gullahs' signature addition to the peas and rice dish called Hoppin' John; see page 160 for recipe); and who can feature cucumbers without dill or potatoes without parsley? My son Logan's top choices are the mints: lemon, 'Chocolate', Vietnamese—he knows them all. Susan loves rosemary and sage and keeps snips of both in her pockets to take out and smell throughout the day. But there are others—savory, chervil, salad burnet—that I introduce clients to at the market, feeling as if I'm handing out great culinary secrets. In the world of food, herbs are a ticket to distant places. They wake us up, and make familiar dishes seem new again. A fresh, ready supply of them will take your cooking to a higher level.

All this, from plants that are among the easiest to grow.

If you've never gardened, start here. Choose some of your flavor favorites and then add some you don't know. You can begin by planting seed trays 2 months before frost danger passes, setting them in a bright, warm spot that gets several hours of direct sun each day, keeping trays well watered, and fertilizing after a month with fish emulsion. In the garden, once the weather has turned, tuck them up in beds with compatible fellows—dill with lettuce, summer savory with onions, chervil with radishes—or give them their own spot, leaving extra space around eager growers like mint.

Many herb-loving gardeners grow them in the vegetable beds *and* in pots around the kitchen door, where they're easy to pinch for cooking and hard to forget to water. With herbs, using them regularly is a form of maintenance—the more you pinch, the more they grow. Their main requirements (since a lot of them are Mediterranean natives) are plenty of sun and well-drained soil—with a pH of 6.5. But some, like the mints and parsley, do fine in part-shade. Pests aren't much of an issue for herbs, which is just one more plus.

Perennial herbs, such as thyme, oregano, and mint, grow outdoors all year in the mild climate of Southern California, but in colder regions must be moved inside for winter, or treated as annuals and replanted each spring. Annuals (basil, cilantro, dill) grow, flower, and go to seed in one season. You can dry and save the seeds, but herb seedlings are so plentiful in spring, in nurseries and farmers' markets, and they grow so fast when you plant them, that many gardeners like to buy and get them in the ground as soon as the weather warms.

MY TOP PICKS

Basil: 'Medinette', 'Sweet Salad', 'Napoletano', 'Purple Bush', 'Spicy Globe', 'Indian', 'Ararat', Thai, Persian **Bergamot:** Lemon, wild, 'Bergamo' **Chamomile:** 'Bodegold' **Chervil:** Curled, 'Brussels Winter' **Cilantro:** Pot, culantro (Mexican), 'Rau Ram' (Vietnamese), 'Santo', 'Papalo', 'Delfino', 'Xiang Cai', 'Jantar' **Dill:** 'Fernleaf', 'Hercules', 'Dukat Super', 'Mammoth', 'Delikat' **Fennel:** Sweet, bronze, 'Grosfruchtiger' **Fennel (bulbous):** 'Florence', 'Perfection', 'Orion' **Lemongrass:** East Indian, West Indian **Marjoram:** Sweet, variegated, wild, 'Zaatar' **Mint:** Lemon, English, Vietnamese, 'Chocolate', Japanese, Swiss, ginger, orange, 'Hillary's Sweet Lemon', nepetella, Yerba Buena **Oregano:** Cretan, Greek, Italian, Syrian, Cuban, Mexican, 'Kaliteri', 'Herrenhausen', 'Zorba Red', 'Turkestan' **Parsley, curled:** 'Green River', 'Starke Triple Curled', 'Forest Green' **Parsley, flat-leaf:** 'Italian Forest', 'Titan', 'Giant Italian', 'Mitsuba' **Parsley root:** 'Hamburg', 'Berliner' **Rosemary:** 'Tuscan Blue', 'Sawyer's', 'Huntington Carpet', 'Beneden Blue', 'Pink Majorca', 'Gorizia' **Sage:** 'Bergarrten', 'Golden', 'Holt's Mammoth', 'Purple', 'White Dalmatian', 'Honey Melon', 'Sage of Bath', 'Grower's Friend', 'Pineapple' **Savory:** 'Promata', Winter, Lemon, 'Midget' **Shiso:** Green, red, Korean **Tarragon:** French, Spanish **Thyme:** English, French, Portuguese, 'Golden Lemon', 'Orange Balsam', 'Orange Spice', lime, 'Nutmeg', lemon

LETTUCE

This is the one that hooks beginners. Just about everyone likes it and it's one of the prettiest edibles, leafing out in rounds, spears, curls, and ruffles, in colors ranging from lime green to speckled red. You can grow lettuce (*Lactuca sativa*) in pots, troughs, or beds and start it from seed or seedlings. It will sprout from seed in 2 to 15 days, in soil temps as low as 40 degrees. Happiest in spring and early summer, it will grow longer if you choose heat-tolerant varieties and harvest them in a timely way.

Lettuce categories are defined by leaf form and growth habit. Romaine, known as Cos, has tall, upright leaves; while butter-head leaves are softer, more tender, and rounded. Crisphead, as its name implies, forms a tightish head as it grows; "leaf" types stay looser. All grow in full sun to part shade and, as summer comes on, appreciate the shelter of larger plants.

If you start with seed, sow it shallowly (⅛ inch deep, 3 to 4 seeds per inch) in good-quality potting soil 3 weeks before you plan to plant outside. A couple of days before you transplant, harden off seedlings by setting them outside during the day and bringing them indoors at night. At the same time, prepare your bed (which should have a soil pH of 6.0 to 7.0) by applying 1 cup of my HayGround fertilizer blend per 10-foot row, watering, and letting the bed sit while your seedlings harden off. Plant seedlings about 10 inches apart (or a bit closer if your bed is small and you need to crowd them), at the same level they occupied in the pot. Alternatively, you can direct-sow lettuce in your beds, as soon as the ground is warm enough to work, starting with cool-weather types like 'Schweitzer's Mescher Bibb', a fetching butterhead. (One caution, though, about planting *too* early: Lettuce exposed to a week of cool

growing temps—below 50 degrees—has a tendency to bolt fast, i.e., shoot upward from the center and get bitter.) As hot weather arrives, switch to varieties that can take it, like 'Amish Deer Tongue' and 'Sweet Valentine'.

Water seedlings deeply, then let the soil dry slightly before you water again. Foliar feed at 3-week intervals, and watch for slugs and snails, which you can combat with Sluggo Plus. Target any green worms that appear with BT.

One of the best ways to keep lettuce from bolting is to use it. You can start by harvesting outer leaves, leaving the center alone, or you can snip off the top 2 or 3 inches, which stimulates growth from the crown. Leaf lettuces will grow back several times after you cut them down almost to the ground (a method also called "cut and come again"). Plant lots of lettuce and experiment. You can't have too much, and if you time it right—starting new seeds in pots as the lettuce grows in your beds—you'll have wonderful salads from spring into fall.

Seed saving with lettuce: Let them go to flower; cut the seed stalks; bag the heads; hang the stalks upside-down in a cool, dry spot to dry; separate out the seeds; and they're ready to plant.

MY TOP PICKS

'Amish Deer Tongue', 'Bunte Forellenschuss', 'Australian Yellow Leaf', 'Bronze Arrowhead', 'Crisp Mint Romaine', 'Drunken Woman', 'Pablo', 'Gold Rush', 'Flame', 'Red Leprechaun', 'Grandpa Admire's', 'Mascara', 'Yugoslavian Red Butterhead', 'Rouge d'Hiver', 'Red Rapids', 'Susan's Red Bibb', 'Sweet Valentine', 'Kwiek', 'Lau's Pointed Leaf', 'Chadwick's Rodan', 'Blonde du Cazard', 'Little Gem', 'Devil's Tongue', 'Sucrine', 'Schweitzer's Mescher Bibb', 'Sanguine Ameliore', 'Demorges Braun'

MELONS

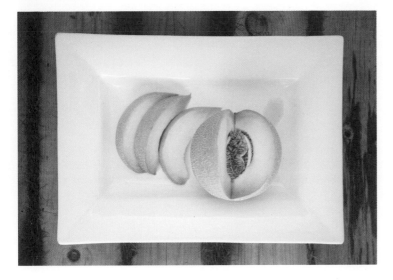

One of my August garden pleasures is watching bees zoom busily around my melon vines, a sight gardeners have enjoyed for thousands of years, in many parts of the world. These sweet, juicy Asian natives like long, hot summers, and they ripen late, so they're a nice reward for months of work, as well as a consolation for the waning of many gardeners' favorite season.

Melons are all part of the family *Cucurbitaceae,* which also includes squash and cucumbers. They need rich, moist soil, with a pH from 6.0 to 6.5; full sun; and lots of heat. In milder regions, you can direct-sow them in your garden bed in spring (after your last frost), first mounding up a mix of soil and organic compost, then planting about 5 seeds around the mound 1 inch deep and 2 inches apart. Later, when plants have 2 sets of leaves, pull out all but the 2 most robust ones.

In harsher climates, it's best to start seeds indoors 3 weeks before your last average frost date, planting seeds ½ inch deep in good-quality potting soil. Once outdoor soil temperatures are at least 60 degrees and before seedlings get pot-bound, transplant them into the garden 2 feet apart on mounded soil, and work ½ cup of my HayGround fertilizer blend into the ground around each.

Keep plants well watered, directing moisture at roots rather than leaves, since melons are prone to fungus, but reduce water as fruit ripens (which makes it sweeter). Hose off any aphids that appear, and control cucumber beetles with spot applications of Pyola. A good way to judge a melon's ripeness is to sniff for its telltale fragrance. Many melons (cantaloupe, for example) change color as they ripen, and some (honeydew) yield slightly at the blossom end when you press on them gently.

Melons cross-pollinate easily if you plant several types, so it will be hard to guarantee seed purity. If you grow only one type, though, and want to save seeds, let a single magnificent melon get somewhat overripe (it will have more seeds that way), then cut it open, separate the seeds from the pulp, and rinse and dry them on paper towels in a cool, shady spot before storing.

MY TOP PICKS
'Canoe Creek Colossal', 'Early Silverline', 'Collective Farm Woman', 'Charantais', 'Banana', 'Coban Orange Flesh', 'Tigger', 'Amish', 'Kin Makuma', 'Petit Gris de Bennes', 'Early Hanover', 'Boule d'Or'

MISCELLANEOUS GREENS

Most leafy greens, such as spinach, arugula, mâche, cress, sorrel, dandelion, escarole, and a number of mustards, are cool-season crops that do best if you plant them in spring or late summer (for fall harvest), since they can handle some frost. If you start seeds indoors (¼ inch deep and 1 inch apart), they'll germinate in 2 to 15 days, in soil ranging from 45 to 70 degrees, with a pH between 6.0 and 7.0.

In spring, after your last hard frost, prepare the bed by digging down 1 foot, loosening soil, and mixing in 1 cup of my HayGround fertilizer blend per 10-foot row. Transplant seedlings 4 to 6 inches apart and keep them moist. If birds attack them, cover rows with garden fabric until plants get established. Should aphids appear, control them with blasts from a hose or, in extreme cases, applications of Pyola.

Harvest leaves when they're young and tender, to stimulate more growth. You can replace plants that grow rangy or go to seed with new seedlings, adding a scant handful of fertilizer each time, to ensure that fresh crops keep coming. To discourage disease, use clean tools and rotate your greens to different beds each year. For seed saving, let plants flower and form seed heads, then hang these upside-down out of the sun to dry.

MY TOP PICKS
Spinach: 'Giant Winter', 'Samish', 'Renegade', 'Bloomsdale', 'Giant Noble', 'Red Malabar **'Arugula:** 'Olive-Leaved Sylvetta', 'Katie', 'Astro' **Escarole:** 'Natacha', 'Eros', 'Rhodos' **Mâche:** 'Gros Graines', 'Vit' **And:** 'Georgia Southern' (Creole) greens; 'Southern Giant' mustard; curled, Persian, 'Upland', 'Cressida', and 'Presto' cress; 'Ruby Streak' mustard; mizuna (Japanese mustard); 'Red-Veined' and French sorrel

MISCELLANEOUS ROOT VEGETABLES

I can't imagine fall and winter meals without rutabagas (*Brassica napus*), parsnips (*Pastinaca sativa*), and turnips (*Brassica rapa*). They're cool growers that produce lots in loose, well-worked soil (with a pH of 6.0 to 6.5), amended with organic compost.

Plant seeds or seedlings; parsnips in early May and rutabagas two weeks later, for fall harvest. Turnips can be planted twice, in mid-April for spring picking and in the beginning of August for fall.

Dig your bed deeply before planting, working in 3 to 4 inches of compost and aged manure and 1 cup of my HayGround fertilizer blend per 5-foot row. Space seedlings 4 inches apart, rutabagas twice that, and water thoroughly and consistently throughout summer. Handpick weeds, and control leaf miners by pinching off blistered-looking leaves. Using floating row covers keeps several other root-crop pests at bay.

Pull turnips when they're good sized but still tender, and dig up rutabagas and parsnips in late autumn. To save turnip seeds in warm-winter climates, leave a plant or two in the garden until they bloom the following spring, and the pods dry enough to make seed removal easy. (In colder areas, lift and overwinter plants, then replant in spring.) For parsnips and rutabagas, let plants linger in the garden through the winter, and they will flower and produce seed heads when the weather warms.

MY TOP PICKS
Parsnips: 'Hollow Crown', 'Cobham Marrow', 'Harris Model' **Rutabagas:** 'Wilhelmsburger', 'American Purple Top', 'All Sweet', 'Angela' **Turnips:** 'Golden Ball', 'Purple Top White Globe', 'White Egg', 'Purple Top Milan', 'Navet des Vertus Marteau', 'Amber Globe', 'Hakurei'

Along with corn and potatoes, okra showed up often on the Williams table when I was a child, and it's still one of my summer favorites. As in the case of my family's own 'Goosecreek' tomato, its seeds arrived in America from the West Indies on a slave ship and were planted a lot around Charleston. Okra thrived in the southern heat and starred in local dishes like gumbo. Cut up in soups and stews, it thickens the broth, though one of the best ways to cook okra (*Abelmoschus esculentus*) is to sauté it whole until the pods are just about to pop open and serve it over rice.

Okra does best in hot, humid climates, with a temperature between 70 and 90 degrees, in soil with a pH of 6.0 to 6.8. Since it has a tough seed coat, I soak the seeds in a bio-stimulant solution (see page 72) overnight before planting. If you start them indoors, plant in trays ¼ inch deep and 1 inch apart 3 to 5 weeks before your average last frost date. Prepare your garden bed by topping it with 2 to 3 inches of bagged leaf mold and working that into the soil before planting seedlings 12 to 18 inches apart and about 1¼ inches deep. Finish the bed with a layer of compost to keep soil warm and hold in moisture. After plants have been growing outside for about 3 weeks, work ½ cup of blended organic fertilizer (my HayGround blend or the equivalent) into the soil around each one.

Let soil dry out between waterings and avoid watering leaves, since okra is susceptible to fungal diseases. Keeping tools clean and rotating crops helps too. Harvest the pods often when they're still tender and 3 to 5 inches long (if you let them get much larger, they will be tough and fibrous).

If you're growing several kinds of okra in a small garden, or if neighbors within a ¾-mile radius of your garden are growing okra, seed purity is a challenge, because the plants are easily cross-pollinated by bees. Saving seeds, though, is a simple matter of letting pods stay on the plant until they start to split, picking out the seeds, and letting them dry.

MY TOP PICKS
'Alabama Red', 'Cowhorn', 'Jimmy T', 'Jing Orange', Thai, 'Bowling Red', Burmese

THE ONION FAMILY

Picture a boisterous crowd of relatives with big personalities, and you've got the *Alliums:* onions, shallots, scallions, garlic, leeks, and chives. Their flavors are strong, as are their scents, which is why they deter a lot of insects and so are good to sprinkle in around your garden. Of course, they're *useful* too. Almost all of my favorite soups and sauces start with garlic and onions on a chopping board. Even their "scapes" (the flower clusters that form on their stem tops) are delicious, thrown in a blender with olive oil, salt, and pepper and spread on toast, asparagus, or baked potatoes.

There are a few tricks to growing onions. One is to choose varieties that do well where you live. Ask your local Cooperative Extension office for a list. In general, "northern" or "long-day" onions are best in cooler climates where days are much longer in summer than winter, and "southern" or "short-day" onions are for warmer, southern climates where day length fluctuates less. Another factor for success is providing onions with loose, fertile soil with a pH of 6.0 to 6.8. Because they like nitrogen, they fit well in a bed where you've recently grown peas or beans.

You can start onions three ways: from seeds, seedlings, or "sets"—small, dried bulbs you can mail order or buy at garden centers in late winter. Sets and seedlings (also available via mail order) give you the jump on growing, especially with big-bulb onions that can take a long time to develop fully.

If you want to start seeds indoors, plant them densely (¼ inch apart or less and ¼ inch deep) in flats full of fresh, good-quality potting soil at least 8 weeks before your area's last average frost date. Put them in a warm spot where temperatures remain fairly even and keep them moist. When their green tops reach 5 inches, cut them back to 3 inches, and continue to do this until it's time to plant them out. Prepare your bed by digging and amending it thoroughly, loosening the soil 1 foot deep, and adding lots of organic compost. Since root crops appreciate bonemeal, work in 2 cups of that per 5-foot row as well. Next, push the soil aside to a depth of 1 to 2 inches and lay down ½ cup of my HayGround fertilizer blend per the same 5-foot row. Cover with soil, then plant seedlings ½ inch deep.

Plant sets or purchased seedlings the same way. Garlic and shallots are easily planted from bulbs (in northern gardens in spring, southern in autumn); just pull apart the cloves and plant them points up, an inch or 2 deep and 4 inches apart.

You can also grow these easy characters in a pot, watering well but letting them dry out slightly before watering again. If you're growing multiple onion types, they will cross-pollinate, but not with leeks or chives. To save seeds, let the plant flower and the scapes dry before cutting them off and hanging them upside-down to dry further, ideally with a paper bag tied around scapes to catch the seed.

MY TOP PICKS
Chives: Garlic, 'Grolau', 'Grande' **Garlic:** 'Bogatyr', 'Chet's Italian Red', 'German Extra Hardy', 'Russian Giant', 'Inchelium Red', 'Georgian Fire', 'Tochliavri' **Leeks:** 'Carentan', 'Giant Musselburgh' **Onions:** Australian brown, 'Red of Florence', 'Texas Early Grano', 'Yellow of Parma', 'Tropeana Lunga', 'Red Beard', 'He Shi Ko', red Creole, French red **Scallions:** 'Red Beard', Japanese **Shallots:** Dutch yellow, French, gray, 'Frog's Leg'

PEAS

My advice for parents of children who refuse to eat vegetables is always the same: Plant peas. Among the earliest of spring crops, they're fascinating to watch as they grow, shooting up fast and producing tiny pods that swell pleasingly with their sweet, plump cargoes. What a treat it is to wander among the vines, popping open those pods and gobbling peas! In my experience, no child can resist it, and ever afterward, they're more open to all things green.

Like beans, peas *(Pisum sativum)* are givers, boosting soil nitrogen for the plants that follow them. They grow best in well-drained soil (with a pH between 6.0 and 6.7) in full sun. The three main types include pod peas, sugar snaps, and snow peas. The vining types of all three need to grow on teepees or other supports. Pod and snow peas also come in bush varieties.

At planting time (as soon as the ground is warm enough to work), inoculate seeds as you do with beans, to increase yield, sturdiness, and disease resistance. Water starter pots or garden beds first, and plant seeds 1 inch deep, topping with a pinch of inoculant and covering with soil. Space plants 18 to 24 inches apart, and dress around them with bonemeal and my HayGround fertilizer blend, 1 cup of each per 5-foot row.

Keep pea beds moist and weed free (2 inches of a good organic mulch helps with both), practice good garden hygiene, and direct water at roots, not leaves, to head off mildew and fusarium wilt. Watch for leafhoppers, mites, and other pests, and contact your Cooperative Extension office for advice on specific ways to control them in your region.

Harvest peas when they're young and tender, but let the ones you want to save dry on the vine.

MY TOP PICKS

English garden peas: 'Alaska', 'Wando', 'Lincoln', 'Tall Telephone', 'Blauschokker Purple' **Snow and snap peas:** 'Mammoth Melting', 'Golden Sweet', 'Oregon Sugar', 'Weggisser', sugar snap, 'Sugar Ann', 'Sugar Sprint'

PEPPERS, SWEET AND HOT

To me, peppers are the life of the party, in the garden and on the table. Against a green background, they add fiery tongues of red and heart-shaped oranges and golds, like ornaments on the stem. Hot-flavored types wake up the palate; sweeter ones refresh it with their irresistible, juicy crunch.

To grow peppers *(Capsicum)* well, you need to know these things: They need lots of heat and evenly moist soil with a pH between 6.0 and 6.8. Even if you have no garden, you can raise peppers in pots, as long as they're warm and well watered.

Start them indoors as early as 8 to 10 weeks before frost ends in your region, planting them ½ inch deep in small containers or trays of top-grade potting mix and keeping them in a bright room that's around 70 degrees during the day and at least 60 degrees at night. (Setting trays on heating pads is ideal, since germination is best at soil temps from 70 to 85 degrees.)

Once seedlings have 2 robust sets of leaves, move them up to 4-inch pots and feed them with a dose of liquid fertilizer. I recommend making your own using these ingredients, all available on the Internet: ½ cup of undiluted worm tea, 4 tablespoons of the bio-stimulant Agri-Gro, ½ teaspoon of the wetting agent ThermX 70, and 2 teaspoons of nitrogen-rich fish emulsion. Mix them all into ½ gallon of water to make a solution and use it immediately, applying whatever is left over around other plants throughout your garden—edibles, shrubs, even roses.

It's important to wait on transplanting peppers outside until the days warm to 60 degrees and the nights are above 50. Prepare your bed by working in more nitrogen in the form of fishbone meal (about 8 cups per 4-by-6-foot bed). Space seedlings 12 to 18 inches apart, and top-dress the soil around each with ½ cup of my HayGround fertilizer blend.

As your peppers grow, watch for the same pests that like tomatoes, controlling worms with BT and blasting aphids with a hose.

Seed saving is tricky, since peppers cross easily with one another. Many small-space gardeners lack the room to isolate peppers enough to keep seeds pure. You can always save seeds and see what you get, of course, scooping them out of the peppers at picking time and drying them on paper in a cool, shady spot before storing.

MY TOP PICKS

Hot peppers: 'Aji', 'Chocolate Habanero', black Hungarian, 'Fatali', 'Fish', 'Georgia Flame', 'Habanero Mustard', 'Red Savina', 'Squash', 'Lemon Drop', 'Jamaica Scotch Bonnet', 'Habanero Gold', 'Scotch Bonnet Burkina Yellow', 'Scotch Bonnet Chocolate', 'Manzano Yellow', purple jalapeño **Sweet peppers:** 'Beaver Dam', 'Alma Paprika', 'Buran', 'Chocolate Beauty', 'Chervena Chushka', 'Jimmy Nardello's', 'Quadrato d'Asti Giallo', 'Sheepnose Pimento'

POTATOES

Potatoes *(Solanum tuberosum)* are New World natives that appeared *a lot* at dinnertime as I was growing up. They're filling, they go a long way when you're feeding a big family, and they're versatile—delicious cooked a hundred ways, including simply baked whole, sliced open, and anointed with butter and salt. Many of the heirloom varieties we raise today were developed following the 1840s Irish Potato Famine, when farmers all growing more or less the same tubers had their crops wiped out by a killing blight.

Even now, *where* you garden is key to which potatoes you grow, so consult your Cooperative Extension office about which varieties do well in your region. Mail-ordered seed potatoes come as egg-sized or larger tubers that you either plant whole (the smallest ones) or cut into chunks with at least one eye per piece.

Three weeks before your average last frost date, work 2 cups of bonemeal into every 10 feet of your garden bed, which should contain fresh, top-quality potting soil. (Potatoes prefer a pH between 6.0 and 7.0.) Plant seed potatoes or chunks 4 to 6 inches deep, leaving 1 foot between them and 12 to 32 inches between rows, depending on how much space you have. When plants sprout up to about 8 inches, mulch them thickly with aged, organic compost, mounding it up around their stems but leaving tops free. If you do this at least one more time when plants grow up again 8 inches, you'll help protect the developing tubers against sunscald as they push up through the soil. (You can also, if you're space-challenged, grow your spuds in a big, deep pot.) Keep soil evenly moist and guard against the Colorado potato beetle with weekly applications of insecticidal soap. If you see the bugs, you can also spot-spray with Pyola. Viruses and wilts can plague potatoes too, and your only recourse is to get rid of the affected plants (though never in your compost pile).

When plants die down, that's often a sign that they're ready to harvest. If they're still growing strong, though, and you know (by digging up a potato) that they're ready to take, cut off the plant foliage yourself. Before harvesting, let the tubers stay in the ground a couple of weeks beyond the cutting or the dieback, which boosts their storage life. To prolong it further, keep potatoes in a cool, dim, moist place with good air circulation until you're ready to eat them.

If you like the potatoes you've grown, you can easily propagate them by cutting them up and replanting pieces with eyes, as I've described above. You can also store your seed potatoes, again in a cool, dark spot. Then, a few weeks before you plan to plant them, place them in warmer, brighter conditions and let them sprout, so they'll develop faster once they're in the ground.

MY TOP PICKS
'Yukon Gold', 'Island Sunshine', 'Cranberry Red', 'Onaway', 'All Blue', 'Rose Gold', 'Caribe', 'Russian Banana', 'Rose Finn Apple', 'Swedish Peanut'

RADISHES

While gardening in general demands patience, radishes don't. Within a matter of days, they sprout from seeds sown directly in garden beds, and maybe 3 weeks later, they're ready to pull, wash, and pop in your mouth. For sheer speed, ease of growing, and the buried-treasure aspect of their harvest, they're a great crop to plant with kids. And there are so many kinds! 'French Breakfast' is a white-tipped red with an elongated shape. Round 'Easter Egg' features many colors in one crop: whites, reds, and pinks. Japanese 'Daikon' is long and creamy. 'China Rose' looks like a stubby pink finger.

Partial to cooler weather, radishes (*Raphanus sativus*) will nevertheless produce pretty much from spring into fall, suffering most in peak summer heat. Some (like 'Crimson Giant') are more heat tolerant than others, while certain ones ('China Rose', 'Philadelphia White Box') are really best as autumn or even winter choices. The fact is, though, that radishes develop and mature so fast that they're in and out of a bed quickly, especially if you harvest them in a timely way, when they're young, tender, and mild-tasting. Many gardeners plant radish

seeds every couple of weeks during the growing season, to ensure a continuous supply.

Since they tend to like fertile soil (with a pH between 6.0 and 7.0), work generous amounts of compost into the top few inches of your bed before you plant. Draw a ½-inch-deep furrow along the bed with a spade or your finger and drop in seeds about 1 inch apart. Keep them well watered, and plant some garlic nearby to discourage root maggots.

MY TOP PICKS
'Red Watermelon', 'Zlata Yellow', 'French Breakfast', 'Daikon', 'Icicle Short', 'Easter Egg', 'Bartender Red Mammoth', 'Misato Green', 'China Rose', 'Noir Gros Rond d'Hiver', 'Pink Beauty'

RASPBERRIES AND BLACKBERRIES

An investment in a garden's future, a raspberry or blackberry patch showers big rewards on those who don't mind waiting. Raspberries are the hardier choice for gardeners in cooler climates, while blackberries do better in warmer ones. Both plants (classified botanically as *Rubus*) can fruit for years. But though their roots are perennial, their canes last only for 2 years, growing and leafing out during their first season, overwintering, then fruiting and dying the following summer. Everbearing raspberries, the exception, fruit in autumn on first-year canes and then again the summer after that.

Site your berry patch in a full-sun but wind-sheltered spot with good drainage, avoiding beds where, during the previous 4 years, you have had tomatoes, peppers, potatoes, or eggplant—edibles that raise the threat of soil-borne verticillium wilt. Shop for plants at a top-quality nursery that sells guaranteed virus-free plants.

Before planting in spring, after hard-frost danger has passed, dig lots of organic compost into your soil (which should have a pH between 5.6 and 7.0), and space plants

3 to 5 feet apart. Provide supports or trellises for raspberries. Keep your bed well watered and weeded, and lay down 3 inches of organic mulch (something like hay or pine needles) to hold moisture and discourage weeds.

Cut out spent summer-fruiting canes in autumn and any others that look damaged or diseased. At the same time, tie the fresh new canes onto trellises or wire supports in order to keep them from sprawling on the ground and growing out of control.

To get a strong fall crop from everbearing raspberries, cut canes to the ground in spring. Harvest raspberries when they easily come off the canes and blackberries when they've darkened and sweetened. If birds are beating you to your berries, cover plants with protective netting.

MY TOP PICKS
Blackberries: 'Black Satin Thornless', 'Ebony King', 'Chester'
Raspberries: 'Heritage Red', 'Anne', 'Royalty Purple', 'Logan Black', 'Fallgold', 'Brandywine Purple', 'Jewel'

SQUASHES

Summer and winter squashes and pumpkins all belong to the plant genus *Cucurbita,* and all have long been important edibles in New World cultures. Many were native to Central America and Mexico, and from there traveled to North America, where they were incorporated into Native American cooking. The word "squash" comes from an Algonquin Indian word that means "eaten raw," or unripe.

Pick summer squashes in an immature stage, while their seeds and skin are still tender. Leave winter squashes, including pumpkins, on the vine to ripen, and even after harvesting, store them further to eat during the cold months. There are vining squashes, which must be grown on trellises, and bush types, which need no support but do best, as all squashes do, when planted on mounds. Squashes are full-sun plants and prefer fertile soil with a pH between 6.0 and 7.0.

Start seeds indoors in pots 3 weeks before your average last frost date, sowing them 1 inch apart and ¼ inch deep. Before transplanting out, create mounds in your beds with a mix of good potting soil and organic compost. For bush varieties, mounds should be 1 foot tall and 3 to 4 feet across, and you'll plant 2 to 3 seedlings 1 foot apart on each, working in 1 cup of my HayGround fertilizer blend around each plant. For vines, create 1-foot-tall mounds adjacent to support walls or trellises, and space plants 1 foot apart, fertilizing as above. Since squash plants bear both male and female flowers and require insect pollination, spacing them close together makes it more likely that visiting bees will hit multiple blooms on several plants and thereby increase the fruit set.

Water regularly during summer heat, directing moisture at root zones rather than leaves to head off fungal problems. Watch for squash beetles and vine borers, targeting them with applications of Pyola. Pick summer squashes when they're young and tender; let winter squashes stay on the vine until you have to work to force a fingernail through the rind. (If you cut winter squashes and include an inch of stem, they'll be sweeter.)

Squashes belonging to the same species cross-pollinate easily, so if you grow them close together, their seeds won't come true. If you're growing different species, you can save their seeds by letting a few fruit mature beyond the ripe stage, until just before they begin to rot, removing the seeds and drying them out of the sun.

MY TOP PICKS

Summer squashes: 'Nimba' zucchini, 'Yugoslavian Finger Fruit', 'Wood's Bush Scallop', 'Yellow Crook', 'Golden Sunshine', 'Black Beauty', 'Costata Romanesco', 'Pattison Panache Jaune et Vert', 'Striata d'Italia', 'Zucchetta' **Winter squashes:** 'Australian Butter', 'Long Island Cheese', 'Guatemalan Blue Banana', 'Kikuza', 'Iran', 'Fordhook Acorn', 'Marina di Chioggia', 'Cornfield Pumpkin', 'Queensland Blue', 'Musquee de Provence', 'Sibley' (also known as 'Pike's Peak'), 'Thelma Sanders', 'Pennsylvania Dutch Butter Crookneck'

STRAWBERRIES

Grow them in a pot! Plant them as edgers in a flower bed! Whatever you do, don't miss out on the sweetness of strawberries *(Fragaria),* for many of us the defining summer fruit. Their jammy scent takes me back to the fun of hunting them down under leaves, like hidden jewels. A sun-warmed bowl is my version of heaven.

The three main strawberry types include June bearers, which crop generously once, early in the season; everbearers, which produce twice; and "day-neutral" varieties, which flower and fruit throughout summer into fall. Your Cooperative Extension office can help you choose the right ones for your climate, as can a visit to a good local nursery that sells certified, disease-free plants.

You can buy and plant strawberries (which prefer a soil pH between 5.8 and 6.2) as soon as the ground is warm enough to work in spring and danger of hard frost has passed. Pick a spot in full sun and dig down 6 to 8 inches, loosening soil and working in several inches of organic compost and about 1 pound of bonemeal per 4-by-6-foot bed. As with raspberries,

to lower the risk of verticillium wilt, avoid planting where you've previously grown potatoes, tomatoes, peppers, or eggplant. Set plants just deep enough in the ground to cover their roots, 8 inches apart, and snip off any runners to boost fruit production. Water regularly, and, during their first year, pinch off all the blooms of June bearers when they appear, and of other varieties until July 1. (Again, you will eventually get more fruit.)

Weed your new patch faithfully, and watch for pests, blasting aphids with a hose and applying Sluggo to control slugs. In fall, prune off old foliage, and before winter sets in, mulch the bed thickly with straw. In spring, spread a 1-inch layer of your own organic compost around each plant to provide supplemental nutrients.

MY TOP PICKS
'Ogallala', 'Quinault', 'Giant Robinson', 'Ozark Beauty', 'Dunlap'

SWEET POTATOES AND YAMS

Many people are confused over the distinction between these two, which resemble each other and are often referred to interchangeably. But sweet potatoes (*Ipomoea batatas*) are close relatives of the American morning glory, while yams, native to Africa and Asia, belong to the genus *Dioscorea*. Yams came to the United States on slave ships, as food for their captive cargoes. Once here, the slaves ate sweet potatoes too, calling these similar, starchy tubers *nyami,* or yams.

Though you also grow them similarly, it's hard to find true yam seeds, so you'll probably opt for sweet potatoes. Start these by burying the whole tuber 2 inches down (in the ground in mild climates; in an indoor pot where spring is frosty) and then planting what sprouts. Break the sprouts off the potato and plant it in a container until it develops roots, if there's still danger of a frost. Otherwise, plant it in the garden, in soil (with a pH between 6.0 and 7.0) that you have prepared by working in a 3-inch layer of organic compost and 1 cup of bonemeal for each plant. Set slips in a 12- to 20-inch-deep trench, spacing them 16 to 18 inches apart and filling in

and mounding the soil as plants develop, though always leaving 12 inches of foliage showing. Pests are rarely a problem.

Water well, especially in dry spells, and harvest when summer heat wanes, digging down carefully so as not to harm skins, which makes them harder to store. Put them somewhere warm and dry for a week or two, then store in a coolish (50- to 60-degree) place that gets plenty of air.

MY TOP PICKS

Sweet potatoes: 'Centennial', 'Nancy Hall', 'Golden Jewel', 'Vardaman', 'Puerto Rico' (vineless), 'Southern Queen' **True yam varieties (if you can find them):** 'Guinea', 'Congo Yellow', 'Purple Ceylon', Chinese *(Dioscorea alata)*

TOMATOES

Everyone wants them! The vegetable gardener's holy grail, tomatoes are, for so many people, a powerful taste memory from bygone years—when a neighbor or relative grew them, and their round, plump forms were the bright beacons of high summer. Nothing matches the brimming sweetness of fresh tomatoes, especially not the dry supermarket types, bred to endure the shipping and handling that thinner-skinned heirlooms can't take. Many of my clients say they can't resist eating their way through the tomato patch, some carrying a salt shaker permanently in a pocket of their favorite gardening pants.

I confess to being an avid tomato grazer myself. I love their sun-warmed juiciness, and the variation in flavors as I move from plant to plant. I'm intrigued by the story of the tomato,

Lycopersicon lycopersicon, a South American native that traveled to Europe and became a cultivated garden crop there a couple of centuries before North Americans ate it. (In fact, maybe because it's part of the nightshade family, it was long considered poisonous here.)

There are so many wonderful tomatoes that it's fun to try new ones every year. True, there are some I can never be without, for example, my own family's heirloom from the Caribbean via South Carolina, 'Goosecreek', a medium-sized dark red with a very rich, fruity flavor. This is an "indeterminate" type, meaning that the plant keeps growing and producing from its first fruit (ready to pick 75 to 80 days after you start the seed) until frosty weather sets in. "Determinate" tomatoes—such as 'Fargo', a 2-inch yellow, and 'Ida

FROM SEED TO SKILLET

Gold', a bright-orange fruiter—develop on shorter vines and ripen all at once. Especially fast growers like 'Siberia', which produces in only 48 days, are referred to as early tomatoes, while others ('Dinner Plate', for instance) can take up to 100 days to ripen. Another way to categorize tomatoes is by size (the ½-ounce 'Golden Cherry' vs. the 4-pound 'Big Zac'), and another is by use: Smallish 'Lime Green Salad' and 'Tuscany' are perfect sliced with fresh lettuce; 'Pink Brandywine' and 'Giant Belgium' are gorgeous fanned on a plate with mozzarella; 'Amish Paste' and 'Opalka' make particularly good sauces.

Hardly difficult to grow, tomatoes have certain preferences that set them apart from other edibles. Give them hours of sun and a little extra attention, and they will pay you back with extra-bountiful crops free of characteristic tomato problems.

I highly recommend starting tomatoes either from seed in pots or as seedlings in beds. You can start seeds indoors, planting them ¼ inch deep and 2 inches apart, 6 to 8 weeks before your region's average last frost date, and keeping soil evenly moist by covering pots or trays with a grow-dome or plastic. Once the first set of serrated leaves has developed, you can either transplant to a bigger pot, immersing the stem in the potting mix to a level just below the first leaf pair, or, if the weather's mild enough, set plants out in your beds. Tomato seedlings appreciate a soil pH of 6.5. Whether you grow your own or buy seedlings, before planting them out, strip off the immature leaves that lie lower on the stem than the serrated pair. My grandmother used to put these stripped leaves in the hole, then bury the seedling's stem up to that first true set.

At transplanting time, I like to dress the soil around each plant—even if I'm planting in a raised bed in great-quality potting soil—with ¼ cup of my HayGround fertilizer blend. I repeat this application when I begin to spot pea-sized tomatoes, and at that point, I also top the tomato bed with 2 inches of my own organic compost to help retain moisture and add minerals. Other than that, I don't fertilize further except to foliar feed every 10 to 14 days, with ½ cup of worm tea plus 4 tablespoons of Agri-Gro mixed into 1 gallon of water.

There is a certain amount of controversy related to tomato spacing and pruning. Some gardeners insist on giving each plant a wide margin of space, as well as pruning its center liberally, to promote air circulation and discourage fungus. In my experience, tomatoes don't mind being crowded if you train them (with twist ties or string) up a sunny wall or fence, where you can space them 1 foot apart. Giving vines support and pruning their lower parts to ensure that neither foliage nor fruit touches the ground helps keep them fungus free, as does avoiding getting water on their leaves.

If you cage plants to support them, leave 3 feet between each. Or you can twine them up teepees, or grow individual plants in wide pots at least 2 feet deep. (Tomatoes, particularly smallish ones, thrive in pots.) Thinning fruit, I have found, is unnecessary, since plants tend to drop enough of their own weak or undeveloped fruit to leave the stronger ones to grow larger.

Let plants dry a bit between waterings (until soil feels dry 2 inches down), and, as fruit ripens, water even less (until soil is dry 3 inches down). This will not only head off the excessive wateriness and cracking that tomatoes fall prey to, but it will also increase your plants' yield and intensify the tomatoes' flavor. Don't fertilize any more than I've outlined above, or you risk excessively leafy plants with curling yellow leaves and scant output of fruit.

Seed saving is easy with tomatoes. Take one you want to plant again, cut it in half, and squeeze its seeds and pulp into a plastic container. Add an inch of purified water to the container and let it stand for a couple of days, uncovered, in the shade, until it forms a white coating on top. Strain and wash the seeds, lay them out on a paper towel, pat with a clean cloth, and leave them out in the shade until the paper is completely dry. Store them in a jar or envelope in a cool, dry, dark place until ready to plant.

Most tomato seeds last for at least 2 years. I found some that my grandmother had saved—who knows how long ago?—and they germinated and produced great fruit for me!

MY TOP PICKS

Bi-color or striped: 'Red Zebra', 'Golden Pineapple', 'Ananas Noire' (also known as 'Black Pineapple'), 'Hillbilly Flame', 'Old German', 'Williams Striped', 'Gold Medal' **Black:** 'Chocolate Amazon', 'Paul Robeson', 'Black Prince', 'Black from Tula', 'Nyagous', 'Brown Berry', 'Pierce's Pride', 'Black Cherry' **Green:** 'Moldovan Green', 'Aunt Ruby's German Green', 'Spears Tennessee Green', 'Greenwich', 'Green Pineapple', 'Green Zebra' **Orange:** 'Mango', 'Kentucky Beefsteak', 'Amana Orange', 'Kellogg's Breakfast' **Red:** 'Goosecreek', 'German Red Strawberry', 'St. Pierre', 'Scarlet Topper' (also known as 'Pritchard'), 'Tartar from Mongolistan', 'Cosmonaut Volkov' **Yellow:** 'Yellow Mortgage Lifter', 'Azoychka', 'Wapsipinicon Peach', 'Egg Yolk', 'Great White', 'Dr. Wyche's Yellow'

CHAPTER

9

FROM MY KITCHEN TO YOURS—WILLIAMS FAMILY RECIPES

We come now to the ultimate reward—turning the bounty from the garden into a feast for the table. Here is where I share some of the foods I grew up with, dishes born of my family's Gullah and Shinnecock traditions. I have chosen a few that I remember most fondly and still cook today, especially those that make the best use of the summer and fall harvest: juicy tomatoes, ripe berries, okra, and squash.

SOUPS AND STEWS

GERTRUDE'S LIMA BEAN SOUP

More a stew than a soup, this dish of my mother's was served on a plate, over rice, with pork chops or ham. For me, it was the ultimate comfort food. I always called in advance before I headed home to visit, and asked my mother to make me some.

- 1 POUND DRIED LIMA BEANS, PICKED THROUGH, RINSED, AND SOAKED OVERNIGHT IN COLD WATER
- 3 TABLESPOONS OLIVE OIL
- 2 LARGE ONIONS, CHOPPED
- 2 LARGE SWEET PEPPERS, RED OR ORANGE, CHOPPED
- 4 STALKS CELERY, CHOPPED
- 4 MEDIUM CARROTS, CHOPPED OR GRATED
- 2 CUPS CHICKEN OR VEGETABLE BROTH
- 3 SPRIGS FRESH PARSLEY OR LOVAGE, MINCED SALT AND FRESHLY GROUND BLACK PEPPER
- 1 STRIP BACON, COOKED AND CRUMBLED (OPTIONAL)

Drain and rinse the soaked beans, then bring them to a boil in a soup pot with water to cover, adding more water as needed, and cook until the beans are tender but still hold their shape, about 45 minutes. Drain and set aside in the soup pot.

Heat the oil in a medium skillet and sauté the onions until translucent. Stir in the peppers, celery, and carrots and cook until they begin to soften but are still crisp.

Mix the vegetables into the soup pot with the beans, add the broth, and simmer for 10 minutes.

Season with the parsley, and salt and pepper to taste, and serve with or without a sprinkling of crumbled bacon.

Serves 8 to 10

LAWRENCE'S FISH CHOWDER

Near where I grew up on Long Island, there were natural gla-cial lakes where my brothers and I would fish for large-mouth bass, catfish, and pickerel. We also went clamming, musseling, and crab hunting on local beaches. After a long day of fishing and beachcombing, we'd come home with the goods for my father's special chowder. The dish varied, depending on what we'd brought him, and occasionally, if we hadn't fished and he felt like cooking, he'd go to the docks for fresh-caught cod and shrimp and use those. My sister Thelma passed his secret recipe on to me, and we both still make it, serving it the way he did, with hot biscuits or cornbread right out of the oven.

    6 STRIPS BACON, CHOPPED

    3 CLOVES GARLIC, CRUSHED

    1 CUP CHOPPED ONION

    ¼ CUP ALL-PURPOSE FLOUR

    4 CUPS 1-INCH POTATO CUBES (PEELED OR UNPEELED)

    1 CUP 1-INCH CARROT CUBES

    ⅔ CUP CHOPPED CELERY STALKS AND LEAVES

    2 TEASPOONS SALT (SEASONED OR PLAIN)

    ½ TEASPOON GROUND CAYENNE PEPPER

    ½ TEASPOON RED PEPPER FLAKES

    ½ TEASPOON DILL SEED

    4 WHOLE CLOVES

    3 WHOLE FRESH BAY LEAVES

    2 POUNDS CUBED FRESH FISH FILLETS (COD, HALIBUT,
        SWORDFISH, OR ANY SIMILARLY FIRM-FLESHED FISH)

    1 POUND FRESH CLAMS, MUSSELS, CRAB, OR WHOLE SHRIMP
        (CLEANED AND DEVEINED)

    3 CUPS CANNED EVAPORATED MILK

Fry the bacon in a large, heavy saucepan or soup kettle until crisp. Remove, drain, and reserve.

Add the garlic and onion to the pan and sauté them in the drippings for 5 minutes, until softened. Whisk in the flour until smooth. Add the potatoes, carrots, celery, salt, cayenne, pepper flakes, dill, cloves, bay leaves, and most of the reserved bacon (saving some for garnish). Bring everything to a boil, cover, and simmer until the vegetables are tender, 15 to 25 minutes.

Add the fish and shellfish and simmer until just cooked through, 10 minutes more, stirring occasionally.

Blend in the milk, heat just to boiling, and turn off the heat. Remove the bay leaves and cloves and garnish with the remaining bacon.

Serves 6

VEGETABLE SIDE DISHES

INDIAN SUMMER SUCCOTASH

Succotash, the name of which comes from a Native American word, was eaten by both my mother's and father's sides of the family. The Native American version tends to feature corn, butter beans, and tomatoes cooked in butter. The Gullah version adds okra and onions. But, as with many family dishes in my house, the ingredients varied, depending on what was ready in the garden and who was cooking. Rather than relying on recipes, we all learned to cook by instinct, getting the general gist of a particular dish and then mixing it up according to what felt right. That said, here is my take on a Williams favorite, which goes beautifully with rice.

- 2 TABLESPOONS UNSALTED BUTTER
- 5 MEDIUM YELLOW ONIONS, CHOPPED
- 5 LARGE TOMATOES, CHOPPED
  KERNELS FROM 3 LARGE EARS OF CORN
- 1 CUP FRESH LIMA BEANS OR FROZEN, THAWED LIMA BEANS
- ¼ CUP WATER OR CHICKEN BROTH
  SALT AND FRESHLY GROUND BLACK PEPPER
  GROUND CAYENNE PEPPER
- 1 POUND OKRA, UNCUT

Melt the butter in a heavy skillet over medium heat and fry the onions until tender and translucent.

Add the tomatoes, corn, lima beans, water, and salt, pepper, and cayenne to taste and cook, stirring, for 5 minutes.

Add the uncut okra and continue cooking until the vegetables are tender, about 10 minutes more.

Serves 8

BURNT-ONION COLLARD GREENS

Collards, among the most nutritious greens, were once planted between cotton rows so that hungry insects would attack them and not the cotton. At harvest time, they were picked to feed slaves and (along with other foods like sweet potatoes, grown for the same purpose) became part of the Gullah tradition. Eloise passed this recipe to my mother, who made it often, with pork chops or chicken and cornbread dumplings. For variety, substitute kale, chard, or cabbage for a portion of the collards and add a half pound of whole okra to the pot ten minutes before the greens finish cooking. When the okra pods are on the verge of popping open, the dish is ready to eat.

- ¼ CUP OLIVE OR COCONUT OIL
- 1 LARGE ONION, FINELY CHOPPED
- ½ CUP CHICKEN OR VEGETABLE BROTH
- ¼ CUP DRY WHITE WINE
  SALT AND FRESHLY GROUND BLACK PEPPER
- 2 TO 3 BUNCHES COLLARD GREENS (ABOUT 1½ POUNDS), LEAVES ONLY, WASHED WELL AND CHOPPED

In a heavy skillet, heat the oil slowly over medium-high heat and fry the onion until well browned and blackened a bit around the edges.

Stir in the broth, wine, and salt and pepper to taste, and mix well before adding the chopped greens.

Cook, stirring occasionally, until the greens are tender, 30 to 40 minutes.

Serves 4 to 6

Indian Summer Succotash

Sweet-and-Sour Cucumbers (top), Nana's Creamed Corn (bottom)

SWEET-AND-SOUR CUCUMBERS

Combining tangy and sweet flavors is a popular practice in Southern cooking, and it's a good approach when your garden overflows with cucumbers and you're tired of the usual cold soups and salads with vinaigrette. This recipe, which I've adapted from one of Eloise's, offers the further novelty of briefly boiling the cukes before mixing them into the sweet-and-sour sauce. The result is a zesty summer side dish with a subtle crunch that pairs well with chicken, fish, or pork chops and a green salad.

    5 LARGE CUCUMBERS
  2½ TABLESPOONS UNSALTED BUTTER
  2½ TABLESPOONS ALL-PURPOSE FLOUR
    ½ CUP APPLE CIDER VINEGAR
    ¼ CUP PACKED LIGHT BROWN SUGAR
       SALT AND FRESHLY GROUND BLACK PEPPER
       CHOPPED FRESH DILL

Peel the cucumbers, halve them lengthwise, scoop out the seeds, and cut into 1-inch slices.

Cook in salted, boiling water until barely tender, 5 to 10 minutes. Drain well, reserving 1¼ cups liquid from the pot, before setting the cucumbers aside.

On top of a 2-quart double boiler, melt the butter over high heat and sprinkle in the flour, stirring constantly, until blended. Gradually add the reserved cucumber cooking liquid, the vinegar, sugar, and salt, pepper, and dill to taste; stir to mix.

Add the cucumbers, turn off the heat, cover the pot, and let stand for 30 minutes, stirring occasionally.

Serves 4 to 6

NANA'S CREAMED CORN

Central to the Shinnecock Indian diet, corn was constantly on my family's table in high summer. My brothers and I picked and husked it outside, eating some of it fresh right there in the yard. Then we sat around a big bowl, cutting kernels off the cobs for this wonderful side dish, a specialty of my mother's mother, Nana.

   12 EARS WHITE OR YELLOW CORN
    3 TABLESPOONS ALL-PURPOSE FLOUR
  1½ TABLESPOONS UNSALTED BUTTER, MELTED
    2 TEASPOONS SALT
    2 TEASPOONS SUGAR
    1 TEASPOON FRESHLY GROUND BLACK PEPPER
    2 TABLESPOONS BACON DRIPPINGS OR BUTTER

Cut the kernels from the cobs and transfer them, with their released juices, to a large bowl. With the side of a knife, scrape each cob over the bowl to catch any remaining juice.

Add all the other ingredients except the bacon drippings, mixing well.

Heat the bacon drippings in a large skillet or pot, add the corn mixture, and stir to coat. Bring the mixture to a boil, reduce the heat to low, cover, and simmer until the mixture thickens, 45 minutes to 1 hour.

Serves 8

FRIED OKRA WITH CHIVES

My grandmother Eloise brought this recipe to the family from South Carolina Gullah country, and we ate it often, with rice and meat—pork chops, ham hocks, or chicken. Okra is spectacular fried, brown on the outside and tender inside. By coating the sliced pieces in cornmeal first, you avoid the slimy quality that some people object to. Eloise's recipe called for frying the okra in lard, bacon grease, or butter; the olive oil is my own, healthier modification.

    1 POUND OKRA, CUT INTO ½-INCH PIECES
    ½ CUP YELLOW CORNMEAL
    ½ TEASPOON SALT
    ¼ TEASPOON FRESHLY GROUND BLACK PEPPER
      PINCH OF GROUND CAYENNE PEPPER
    6 TABLESPOONS OLIVE OIL
    1 BUNCH CHIVES, CHOPPED
    ½ CUP CHOPPED RED OR YELLOW ONION (OPTIONAL)

In a paper bag, combine the okra with the cornmeal, salt, pepper, and cayenne and shake to coat.

Heat the oil in a large, heavy skillet over medium heat and fry the okra until it's nicely browned, 15 to 20 minutes. Scoop it into a serving dish, season with more salt and pepper to taste, and sprinkle with the chives and onion, if desired.

Serves 4 to 6

OKRA AND TOMATOES

A common pairing in Gullah and Creole cooking, okra and tomatoes can be a meal in itself if you serve it with the aromatic rice that's grown in the Carolinas. Cooking the okra whole reduces its slimy qualities; slicing it makes for a thicker stew. For a healthier version, use all olive oil in place of butter, and for a spicier kick, add more cayenne.

       ¼ CUP OLIVE OIL
       1 MEDIUM ONION, CHOPPED
       2 CLOVES GARLIC, CHOPPED
6 TO 8 SAUCE TOMATOES, DICED
       ½ CUP CHOPPED FRESH PARSLEY
       ½ TEASPOON SALT
       ½ TEASPOON FRESHLY GROUND BLACK PEPPER
       ¼ TEASPOON GROUND CAYENNE PEPPER
       2 TABLESPOONS UNSALTED BUTTER
       1 POUND OKRA, WHOLE OR SLICED

Warm the oil in a skillet over medium heat and sauté the onion and garlic until soft.

Mix in the tomatoes and cook until tender, then add the parsley, salt, pepper, and cayenne.

Stir in the butter, add the okra, and continue cooking on medium heat until the okra has lost its toughness and the pods (if left whole) are on the verge of popping open, about 10 minutes.

Serves 4 to 6

GREEN BEAN AND
ASPARAGUS CASSEROLE

Essentially a Gullah recipe, this was a perfect summer dish for our Long Island setting, where, throughout my childhood, asparagus grew wild. While a couple of us children would be sent out to gather some, another two were dispatched to the garden for the beans. A bunch of us would then gather around the table under the grape arbor outside and snap the ends off the beans before tossing them in a basket. The smell of this casserole baking takes me back to those times—the afternoon heat, the cool shade, all of us horsing around, making each other laugh, until my grandmother burst out, wondering where her beans were.

4 TABLESPOONS SALTED BUTTER

1 POUND GREEN BEANS, CUT INTO 2-INCH PIECES

½ ONION, FINELY CHOPPED

1 TABLESPOON WHOLE WHEAT FLOUR

1 CUP SOUR CREAM

½ CUP GRATED SHARP CHEDDAR CHEESE

1 TEASPOON SUGAR

½ TEASPOON SALT

⅛ TEASPOON FRESHLY GROUND BLACK PEPPER

2 BUNCHES ASPARAGUS (1½ TO 2 POUNDS), TOUGH ENDS
    REMOVED, CUT INTO 2-INCH PIECES

½ CUP CRUSHED CORNFLAKES

Preheat the oven to 350 degrees F.

Melt 2 tablespoons of the butter in a large saucepan over medium-low heat and cook the beans, stirring, until crisp-tender, about 6 minutes. (If they start to stick, add 2 tablespoons water.) Scoop the warm beans into a small bowl and set aside.

In the same pan, melt another 1 tablespoon butter and sauté the onion until softened.

Add the flour, stirring to blend, then the sour cream, cheese, sugar, salt, and pepper. Continue to stir over low heat until the ingredients are well combined and the cheese is melted.

Mix in the asparagus and the reserved beans and pour the mixture into a buttered, 2-quart casserole dish.

Melt the remaining 1 tablespoon butter and combine it with the cornflakes. Spread this mixture over the vegetables.

Bake uncovered, until lightly browned, about 30 minutes.

Serves 4

Vegetable Rice–Stuffed Tomatoes

MAIN COURSES

GERTRUDE'S EGGS AND RICE

This dish is all about having to feed a lot of kids fast, on not much money! We ate it for breakfast in my house, but in three or four times the quantities that this recipe yields. My mother made it with leftover rice and often added bacon or meat from the night before (ground beef, sausage, hot dogs) to stretch it even further. Whatever we had in the kitchen was fair game, since the basic idea is pretty adaptable. I still make it, usually with brown rice and sometimes chopped cilantro or a pinch of curry.

¼ CUP OLIVE OR COCONUT OIL

1 MEDIUM ONION, CHOPPED

1 RED BELL PEPPER, CHOPPED

2 CLOVES GARLIC, CHOPPED

4 CUPS COOKED LONG-GRAIN RICE (WHITE OR BROWN)

8 LARGE EGGS, BEATEN

½ TEASPOON SALT

¼ TEASPOON FRESHLY GROUND BLACK PEPPER

Heat the oil slowly in a large skillet over medium heat. Add the onion, bell pepper, and garlic. Cook, stirring, until tender, then mix in the rice, eggs, salt, and pepper, and scramble until the eggs are set and everything is well combined.

Serves 4 to 6

GRITS AND SHRIMP CASSEROLE WITH RED PEPPERS, ONIONS, AND TOMATOES

In my family, we all loved grits, a well-known "Southern" food that's made of coarse-ground corn. Originally grits was a Native American dish, and this recipe comes from my Shinnecock grandmother, Nana, who would make it with shrimp she bought fresh from a local boat dock. She always cooked the shrimp last, right in the hot grits; for a thicker, richer sauce, she sometimes added a few slices of sharp Cheddar cheese before serving.

1½ CUPS UNCOOKED WHITE GRITS

½ POUND BACON, DICED

1 CUP FINELY CHOPPED COOKED HAM

2 MEDIUM ONIONS, CHOPPED

2 SMALL RED BELL PEPPERS, CHOPPED

8 LARGE, FRESH TOMATOES, CHOPPED

½ POUND SMALL, FRESH SHRIMP, CLEANED AND DEVEINED

Cook the grits according to the package directions.

Meanwhile, fry the bacon in a medium skillet, until crisp, drain on paper towels, and reserve.

Sauté the ham in the bacon drippings until browned, about 10 minutes.

Add the onions and bell peppers and sauté until tender, 10 minutes more.

Stir the ham and vegetable mixture into the grits pot. Toss the tomatoes and shrimp into the same pot, stir well, and let sit 1 to 2 minutes off the heat to cook the shrimp. Serve topped with the reserved bacon.

Serves 4

VEGETABLE RICE—STUFFED TOMATOES

This dish always reminds me of summer's bounty—of straw baskets heaped with sweet corn, and fat tomatoes that taste best on the day you pick them. Stuffed tomatoes are another Southern favorite, and the rice is a Gullah signature. For added health value, I sometimes substitute long-grain brown rice for the traditional white.

- 6 LARGE FIRM TOMATOES, RED OR GREEN
- 3 TABLESPOONS OLIVE OIL
- 8 LARGE FRESH MUSHROOMS, CHOPPED
- 2 SHALLOTS, FINELY CHOPPED
- 2 CLOVES GARLIC, MINCED
  KERNELS FROM 1 LARGE EAR CORN
- ½ CUP ¼-INCH PIECES THIN ASPARAGUS
- ½ TEASPOON MILD CURRY POWDER
  SALT AND FRESHLY GROUND BLACK PEPPER
- 1 CUP COOKED, LONG-GRAIN WHITE RICE
- ¼ CUP MINCED GREEN OLIVES
- ¼ CUP CHOPPED FRESH BASIL

Preheat the oven to 350 degrees F.

Slice ½ inch off the top of each tomato and set the slices aside.

Scoop out the center of each tomato, leaving ¼ inch all around. Puree the tomato pulp, measure out ½ cup, and reserve the rest for another use. Drain the tomato shells, cut-side down, on paper towels.

Heat the oil in a medium skillet over medium-high heat and sauté the mushrooms, shallots, and garlic for 1 minute.

Add the corn and asparagus and cook for another 2 minutes. Add the tomato puree, curry powder, and salt and pepper to taste, and continue to stir over medium heat until the liquid has almost evaporated.

Stir in the rice, olives, and basil and remove from the heat to cool.

Sprinkle the insides of the tomato shells with more salt and pepper to taste, stuff each one with the rice mixture, and cover with the reserved tomato tops.

Put the tomatoes on an oil-coated baking sheet and bake until the tomatoes soften, 25 minutes.

Serves 4 to 6

HOPPIN' JOHN

A well-known Southern food with African and Caribbean roots, this dish is made by Gullah cooks with small, nutty-tasting brown beans called "cowpeas" or "pigeon peas" (available in African-American neighborhood markets, or online). Other Southerners often substitute black-eyed peas, and sometimes add ingredients like bell peppers and spicy sausages to the traditional mix of rice, beans, and onions, flavored with ham hocks and cayenne. It's a dish served for luck on New Year's Eve, which was always when we ate it, topped with thyme sprigs, but also on many other occasions throughout the year.

- 1 CUP DRIED COWPEAS
- 1 CUP RAW LONG-GRAIN RICE (BROWN OR WHITE)
- ½ POUND SLAB BACON OR 1 HAM HOCK, FINELY DICED
- 1 TEASPOON BACON GREASE OR OLIVE OIL
- 1 TEASPOON SALT
- ¼ TEASPOON FRESHLY GROUND BLACK PEPPER
- ⅛ TEASPOON GROUND CAYENNE PEPPER
- 2 MEDIUM ONIONS, CHOPPED
- 3 TABLESPOONS OLIVE OIL
- 4 TO 6 SPRIGS FRESH THYME

Wash, sort, and soak the cowpeas in water to cover overnight.

Cook the rice according to the package directions.

Fry the bacon in a medium skillet until crisp. Drain on paper towels and reserve.

In a large saucepan, bring 2 quarts of water to a boil. Add the bacon grease, then the pre-soaked peas, salt, pepper, and cayenne, and simmer until the peas are tender but still firm, about 45 minutes.

While the peas cook, sauté the onions in the oil until soft and beginning to brown.

When the peas and rice are done, spoon the rice into the pea pot (1 cup of liquid should remain in the pot; otherwise, add hot water). Heat 2 to 3 minutes on medium, and serve garnished with the onions, bacon, and thyme.

Serves 4 as a main course; 6 as a side dish

Hoppin' John

BREADS AND DESSERTS

SWEET POTATO BISCUITS

The addition of sweet potato gave my Nana's biscuits a distinctive color and sweetness that set them apart from the others we ate—often—in my house. We had hers mainly in the winter, when it was time to use the root crops and squash we had picked in fall and stored in our root cellar. For variety, she sometimes swapped in butternut or acorn squash for the sweet potato.

½ CUP MILK

½ CUP COOKED, MASHED SWEET POTATO

¼ CUP UNSALTED BUTTER, MELTED

¼ CUP SUGAR

1 TEASPOON SALT

¼ ENVELOPE (⅜ TEASPOON) ACTIVE DRY YEAST

2½ CUPS ALL-PURPOSE FLOUR

Heat the milk in a small saucepan until it's just about to boil, then stir in the sweet potato, butter, sugar, and salt. Remove from heat.

Dissolve the yeast in ¼ cup warm water in a big bowl and let it sit for 10 minutes to activate.

Stir the flour and the sweet potato mixture into the dissolved yeast, cover, and let rise in a warm place overnight.

The next day, preheat the oven to 375 degrees F.

Roll out the dough on a floured board to ¾ inch thick. Cut the biscuits with a 2- to 2½-inch biscuit cutter (rerolling the scraps), and put them on a buttered baking sheet to rise again, until almost doubled, ½ hour to 1 hour.

Bake until slightly brown on top, 15 to 18 minutes.

Makes 12 to 18 biscuits

GULLAH CORNBREAD WITH SWEET POTATOES

Cornbread is another food that's common to both traditional Native American and Gullah cooking. In place of the straight cornmeal version my Shinnecock grandmother made, this South Carolina–style bread adds mashed sweet potatoes.

1 CUP FINE YELLOW CORNMEAL

1⅔ CUPS ALL-PURPOSE FLOUR

¼ ENVELOPE (⅜ TEASPOON) ACTIVE DRY YEAST

1 CUP BOILING WATER

2 LARGE EGGS

1 CUP BUTTERMILK

1½ TABLESPOONS UNSALTED BUTTER, MELTED

⅓ CUP COOKED, MASHED SWEET POTATOES

⅓ TEASPOON SALT

In a medium bowl, stir together ⅓ cup of the cornmeal and ⅔ cup of the flour and add ¼ cup warm water (or a little more, if necessary) to form a stiff batter.

Dissolve the yeast in another ¼ cup warm water, let sit for 10 minutes, and blend it into the batter.

Cover the bowl with a kitchen towel and set it in a warm place for several hours, until the contents double in size.

Preheat the oven to 400 degrees F. When the batter has risen, blend the remaining ⅔ cup cornmeal and 1 cup flour in another bowl. Pour the boiling water over them and let cool to room temperature.

continued

Sweet Potato Biscuits

Gullah Cornbread with Sweet Potatoes

Gullah Cornbread with Sweet Potatoes, continued

In a third bowl, beat the eggs, mix in the buttermilk and butter, and stir thoroughly to combine. Add this to the flour mixture, then blend in the yeasted batter, sweet potatoes, and salt.

Bake in a well-buttered 9-by-5-inch loaf pan, or oven-proof pot, checking on the bread after 35 minutes. It's done when the top is golden brown and springs back lightly when touched, about 45 minutes total.

Serve warm, with butter.

Serves 6

WINTER SQUASH BREAD

Another of Nana's recipes, this one again reflects the Native Americans' high esteem for squash, which we grew from spring into fall and stored in our root cellar to eat during the cold months. We loved this bread so much—buttered hot for breakfast or warm from the oven and topped with our hand-cranked vanilla ice cream for dessert—that we would gather around the oven waiting for it to come out! Our whole house filled with its spicy sweetness as it baked, and with twelve hungry children, two loaves were gone in no time. When I make it now, I substitute half whole wheat for the white flour my grandmother used, just to boost its health value a bit.

3 CUPS SUGAR

2 CUPS COOKED, MASHED WINTER SQUASH (BUTTERNUT, ACORN, OR KABOCHA ARE GOOD CHOICES)

4 LARGE EGGS, BEATEN

1 CUP CANOLA OR COCONUT OIL

3½ CUPS ALL-PURPOSE FLOUR

2 TEASPOONS BAKING SODA

2 TEASPOONS SALT

1 TEASPOON BAKING POWDER

1 TEASPOON GROUND CINNAMON

1 TEASPOON GROUND NUTMEG

1 TEASPOON GROUND ALLSPICE

½ TEASPOON GROUND CLOVES

¾ CUP CHOPPED PECANS OR WALNUTS

¾ CUP RAISINS

Preheat the oven to 350 degrees F.

In a large bowl, combine the sugar, squash, eggs, and oil and mix well.

In a medium bowl, combine the flour, baking soda, salt, baking powder, cinnamon, nutmeg, allspice, and cloves. Add them to the squash mixture alternately with ⅔ cup warm water.

Stir in the nuts and raisins and divide the batter between 2 buttered 9-by-5-inch loaf pans. Bake until the bread springs back lightly to the touch, about 1 hour.

Makes 2 generous loaves

Winter Squash Bread

PEACH AND BERRY COBBLER

Fruit cobbler is a familiar Southern dessert, and this Gullah version, which came, of course, from Eloise, combines berries with the more common, straight-peach formula. We always had at least one peach tree when I was a child, and we grew lots of berries—raspberries, blueberries, and blackberries—to supplement those that grew wild in our part of Long Island.

½ CUP UNSALTED BUTTER

2 CUPS SUGAR

¾ CUP ALL-PURPOSE FLOUR

¾ CUP MILK

2 TEASPOONS BAKING POWDER

⅛ TEASPOON SALT

1 CUP SLICED FRESH PEACHES

1 CUP BERRIES OF YOUR CHOICE

CREAM, WHIPPED CREAM, OR VANILLA ICE CREAM
FOR TOPPING

Preheat the oven to 350 degrees F.

Melt the butter in the oven in a deep, 1½-quart casserole dish.

In a medium bowl, combine 1 cup of the sugar, the flour, milk, baking powder, and salt. Pour the batter evenly over the melted butter without stirring.

In a separate medium bowl, mix the peaches and berries with the remaining 1 cup sugar and spoon them over the batter without stirring.

Bake until golden brown, 45 minutes to 1 hour. Serve warm with cream, whipped cream, or ice cream.

Serves 4 to 6

BLUEBERRY SLUMP

We ate this traditional Shinnecock dish, fresh from the oven, for breakfast or as a warm dessert topped with vanilla ice cream. We even had it in winter, when my mother would make it using blueberries she had frozen the previous summer. The term "slump" refers to the fact that the dish tends to fall a bit when spooned out of the pan, and that makes sense to me. I love the smooth tanginess of the blueberries combined with the grainy sweetness of the cornmeal batter.

2 CUPS YELLOW CORNMEAL

1 TEASPOON BAKING SODA

½ TEASPOON SALT

1½ CUPS FRESH BLUEBERRIES OR FROZEN, THAWED BLUEBERRIES

3 LARGE EGGS

1½ CUPS PLAIN YOGURT OR BUTTERMILK

¼ CUP PURE MAPLE SYRUP

Preheat the oven to 425 degrees F.

In a large bowl, combine the cornmeal, baking soda, and salt. Add the blueberries and gently toss together.

In a medium bowl, beat the eggs well, then stir in the yogurt and syrup.

Fold this mixture into the dry ingredients, stirring just enough to combine, with some lumps remaining.

Pour the batter into a buttered 8-by-8-inch baking pan. Bake until the top springs back lightly when touched and is golden brown, about 25 minutes.

Let cool slightly, cut into squares, and serve with or without ice cream.

Serves 4 to 6

Peach and Blueberry Cobbler (top), Blueberry Slump (bottom)

Sweet Pepper Dip

CONDIMENTS AND SAUCES

SWEET-PEPPER DIP

When our peppers ripened in mid-summer, we put them in everything from eggs to soup and we still couldn't eat them fast enough! This dip was Eloise's version of a snack food, and we spread it, slightly warm, on crackers or bread. Sometimes, for dinner, we'd even dip our ribs or chicken in it, we so loved the combination of crispness and sweetness that resulted from cooking half the peppers and leaving half of them raw before blending the two together.

- ¼ CUP OLIVE OR COCONUT OIL
- ¼ MEDIUM ONION, CHOPPED
- 1 CLOVE GARLIC, CHOPPED
- 4 LARGE SWEET BELL PEPPERS, RED AND YELLOW, SLICED INTO STRIPS
- SALT AND FRESHLY GROUND BLACK PEPPER

Warm the oil in a large frying pan and sauté the onion and garlic over medium heat until softened. Add half the sliced peppers and cook until they're very tender.

Let cool slightly, then scrape the contents of the pan into a blender, add the rest of the peppers, and puree until fully smooth. Season with salt and pepper.

Makes about 2 cups

GERTRUDE'S TOMATO SAUCE

My mother's fresh tomato sauce, which she spiced up with a variety of our backdoor herbs as well as chili powder, wasn't just for spaghetti and lasagna. It was the basis of several dishes she made, including red rice and shrimp, and it was also an all-purpose, improvisational tool she used to turn leftovers into brand-new meals. She sometimes added it to okra and tomatoes for extra zest, or she added cooked ground meat and ladled it on rice. It's a great vehicle for the overflow of your tomato harvest, especially oddly shaped or slightly overripe fruit that won't look pretty sliced on a plate.

- 3 TABLESPOONS OLIVE OIL
- 1 LARGE ONION, CHOPPED
- 3 CLOVES GARLIC, MINCED
- 6 LARGE MUSHROOMS, FINELY CHOPPED
- 1 MEDIUM RED BELL PEPPER, FINELY CHOPPED
- 2 LARGE SLICING-TYPE TOMATOES, DICED
- 8 LARGE PLUM TOMATOES, DICED
- 2 SIX-OUNCE CANS TOMATO PASTE
- 1½ TABLESPOONS SUGAR
- 2 TEASPOONS SALT
- 1½ TEASPOONS CHILI POWDER
- 10 FRESH BASIL LEAVES, FINELY CHOPPED
- ¼ TEASPOON CHOPPED FRESH OREGANO
- ¼ TEASPOON CHOPPED FRESH MARJORAM
- ¼ TEASPOON CHOPPED FRESH ROSEMARY
- 2 FRESH BAY LEAVES
- 4 SPRIGS FRESH THYME

Warm the oil in a large saucepan over medium heat and sauté the onion and garlic until translucent.

Add the mushrooms and bell pepper and cook, stirring, for a couple of minutes, then add the fresh tomatoes and stir until they begin to bubble.

Mix in the tomato paste, sugar, salt, chili powder, and herbs. Cover, reduce the heat to low, and simmer until thick and bubbling, about 1 hour.

Uncover, stir, and simmer until further thickened and very fragrant, an additional ½ hour.

Remove the bay leaves and thyme sprigs. The sauce will keep in the refrigerator in an airtight container for up to a week.

Makes about 6 cups

BIBLIOGRAPHY

Ashworth, Suzanne. *Seed to Seed*. Decorah, IA: Seed Savers Exchange, Inc., 1991.

Bartholomew, Mel. *All New Square Foot Gardening*. Franklin, TN: Cool Springs Press, 2006.

Carr, Anna. *Rodale's Color Handbook of Garden Insects*. Emmaus, PA: Rodale, 1979.

Coleman, Eliot. *Four-Season Harvest*. White River Junction, VT: Chelsea Green, 1992.

Creasy, Rosalind. *The Complete Book of Edible Landscaping*. San Francisco: Sierra Club, 1982.

———. *The Edible Herb Garden*. Boston: Periplus Editions, 1999.

Damrosch, Barbara. *The Garden Primer*. New York: Workman, 1988.

Denevan, Jim. *Outstanding in the Field*. New York: Clarkson Potter, 2008.

Don, Monty, and Sarah Don. *From the Garden to the Table: Growing, Cooking and Eating Your Own Food*. Guilford, CT: Lyons Press, 2003.

Ellis, Barbara W. *The Veggie Gardener's Answer Book*. North Adams, MA: Storey Publishing, 2008.

Facciola, Stephen. *Cornucopia II: A Source Book of Edible Plants*. Vista, CA: Kampong Publications, 1998.

Gabor, Brad, and Wayne Wiebe, eds. *Tomato Diseases*. Saticoy, CA: Seminis Vegetable Seeds, Inc., 1997.

Goldman, Amy. *The Heirloom Tomato: From Garden to Table*. New York: Bloomsbury USA, 2008.

Hirsch, David. *The Moosewood Restaurant Kitchen Garden*. Berkeley, CA: Ten Speed Press, 2005.

Jeavons, John. *How to Grow More Vegetables*. Berkeley, CA: Ten Speed Press, 1974.

———. *The Sustainable Vegetable Garden: A Backyard Guide to Healthy Soil and Higher Yields*. Berkeley, CA: Ten Speed Press, 2004.

Loewenfeld, Claire, and Philippa Back. *The Complete Book of Herbs and Spices*. London: David & Charles, 1974.

Lopez, Andrew. *Natural Pest Control: Alternatives to Chemicals for the Home and Garden*. Sebastopol, CA: Harmonious Technologies, 1998.

Male, Carolyn J. *100 Heirloom Tomatoes for the American Garden*. New York: Workman, 1999.

Mikanowski, Patrick, and Lyndsay Mikanowski. *Vegetables: By 40 Great French Chefs*. Paris: Flammarion, 2006.

Morash, Marian. *The Victory Garden Cookbook*. New York: Knopf, 1982.

Pleasant, Barbara, and Deborah L. Martin. *The Complete Compost Gardening Guide*. North Adams, MA: Storey Publishing, 2008.

Pollan, Michael. *Second Nature*. New York: Atlantic Monthly, 1991.

———. *An Omnivore's Dilemma*. New York: Penguin, 2006.

———. *In Defense of Food*. New York: Penguin, 2008.

Raven, Sarah. *Sarah Raven's Garden Cookbook*. London: Bloomsbury, 2007.

Smith, Miranda, and Anna Carr. *Rodale's Garden Insect, Disease & Weed Identification Guide*. Emmaus, PA: Rodale, 1988.

Solomon, Steve. *Gardening When It Counts: Growing Food in Hard Times*. Gabriola Island, BC (Canada): New Society Publishers, 2006.

Vilmorin-Andrieux, MM. *The Vegetable Garden*. London: John Murray, 1885.

Waters, Alice. *Chez Panisse Vegetables*. New York: HarperCollins, 1996.

Weaver, William Woys. *Heirloom Vegetable Gardening*. New York: Henry Holt, 1997.

Zabar, Abbie. *The Potted Herb*. New York: Stewart, Tabori & Chang, 1988.

INDEX

TABLE OF EQUIVALENTS

THE EXACT EQUIVALENTS IN THE FOLLOWING TABLES
HAVE BEEN ROUNDED FOR CONVENIENCE.

LIQUID/DRY MEASUREMENTS

U.S.	METRIC
¼ teaspoon	1.25 milliliters
½ teaspoon	2.5 milliliters
1 teaspoon	5 milliliters
1 tablespoon (3 teaspoons)	15 milliliters
1 fluid ounce (2 tablespoons)	30 milliliters
¼ cup	60 milliliters
⅓ cup	80 milliliters
½ cup	120 milliliters
1 cup	240 milliliters
1 pint (2 cups)	480 milliliters
1 quart (4 cups, 32 ounces)	960 milliliters
1 gallon (4 quarts)	3.84 liters
1 ounce (by weight)	28 grams
1 pound	448 grams
2.2 pounds	1 kilogram

LENGTHS

U.S.	METRIC
⅛ inch	3 millimeters
¼ inch	6 millimeters
½ inch	12 millimeters
1 inch	2.5 centimeters

OVEN TEMPERATURE

FAHRENHEIT	CELSIUS	GAS
250	120	½
275	140	1
300	150	2
325	160	3
350	180	4
375	190	5
400	200	6
425	220	7
450	230	8
475	240	9
500	260	10